WARREN CLAY COLEMAN:
The Leader of the First Black Textile Mill In America

WARREN CLAY COLEMAN:
The Leader of the First Black Textile Mill In America

A clear unsung example of black
enterprise/capitalism after the civil war

Norman J. McCullough, Sr. B.A, M.A.

To order additional copies of this book, contact:
Xlibris
1-888-795-4274
www.Xlibris.com
Orders@Xlibris.com
804711

CONTENTS

Foreword

I had never heard of Warren Clay Coleman until the late 1890s. I knew absolutely nothing of his existence or his accomplishments. It was a coincidence that I was introduced to his name and legacy. I had the good fortune to work at IBM as a computer repairman for many years. After responding to a computer service call in Concord, North Carolina, my customer asked if I had ever heard of Warren C. Coleman. "No" was my answer. She then shared a brief history of Coleman. Andy not only took me to the Coleman Mill, which was less than a mile from her office, but she also showed me the Coleman Historic Marker along Highway 601. Highway 601 has since been renamed Warren C. Coleman Boulevard. I was given a private tour of the entire facility, which was being utilized as a warehouse at the time. To say that I was impressed is an understatement. I was blown away. Never had I heard or fathomed that a person born a slave in the South could rise up from humble and almost impossible odds and achieve so much in such a short period of time.

Now fast-forward to February 2006. I was pasturing a church in Mooresville, North Carolina, and the local AARP asked me to speak to them during Black History Month. I could think of no one better than Coleman to present to the group. I did extensive research. I discovered that Coleman was born in March 1849, one hundred years before I was born. His mother, Roxana, was a mulatto slave on the Coleman plantation in Cabarrus County, North Carolina. His father was Rufus Clay Barringer, who became a lawyer and later a brigadier general in the Confederacy and was a brother-in-law to Stonewall Jackson and D.

H. Hill. My research efforts prompted me to write a book chronicling the life and times of such a driven man. I'm still working on the book.

Fast-forward again to April 2015. I was introduced to Dr. Norman J. McCullough Sr., who is a member and trustee of Price Memorial AME Zion Church in Concord, North Carolina. Dr. McCullough is a New Yorker who makes his home in Concord. Norman is also a teacher of history at RCCC. Once he was introduced to the history of Concord, Coleman, and Price Memorial, he has been on fire to introduce to the entire world this giant of a historic figure. McCullough has traveled to various parts of the country retracing the steps of Coleman to show how he (Coleman) built his various enterprises. Dr. McCullough has conducted Coleman tours throughout Concord showing the Coleman Mill and the neighborhood and gravesite. McCullough has sponsored annual festivals commemorating the life of Coleman, and he has invited me to be a presenter on various occasions to share my knowledge of Coleman. I congratulate and celebrate Dr. McCullough who has appreciated, articulated, and demonstrated his love for the life and legacy of Coleman. This book is a testament to that! God bless you, Dr. McCullough! And the journey continues!

Rev. Thomas D. Lee of Rowan County, North Carolina

Preface

Like so many children of former slaves, I did not know my father. I knew his name because it is on my birth certificate; however, I never met him because my mother married Andrew McCullough, and she did not want me to know about my biological father (John Williams), who was much older than her. My birth certificate indicates that my mother was from the British West Indies (Montserrat) and my biological father was from the Virgin Islands. John Williams was a minister, and my mother was a young girl hoping to find a better life in America. In America, all the people who migrate to this country are looking for a better life. In 1992, I was fortunate enough to take my wife and son to Montserrat (see map of the island on page). It was a blessing because a few years later, a major volcanic eruption took place on the island, and the government could only accommodate people on the south side of the island. Prior to our visit to the islands in the 1990s, in the late '50s and early '60s, my life of living on the Lower East Side of Manhattan with my single mother was at risk. In fact, I was a juvenile at risk, going to my friends' home to eat dinner. And if not for my great aunt and cousin, I would have been another number for the criminal justice system. They came together, at risk to themselves, to assist me to overcome a negative lifestyle that many of the young people living in the Alfred E. Smith projects I knew could not overcome (drugs, gangs, etc.). My family enabled me to complete high school, serve in the army, go on to college, and become a productive, accomplished member of our society. As a first-generation American, I have been able, due to the efforts of my family and many other people, to service and positively impact thousands of adults and youth. Given my background, I see myself in Warren C. Coleman—overcoming the odds and working for the greater good in spite of the obstacles thrown in our way. Others like myself continue to give back so that our youth can take on the mantle and make way for future generations, if we don't burn up the planet.

Acknowledgments

As I write my second book, I must acknowledge so many people who assisted me and made my life possible. Specifically, my family—Darnelle McCullough, Norman J. McCullough Jr., Gloria McCullough, Leona Barzey, Lillian Barzey, and many others—with the 100 Black Men; the Calvary United Methodist Church–Roselle of East Orange, New Jersey; and too many others too numerous to mention. I also want to thank all the members of AME Zion Church in North Carolina and other parts of the country and the members of the Cabarrus County Library on Union Street.

Chapter One

Feeling the Hand of God

I am a descendent of Africa.

—Peter Williams

Traveling to North Carolina

As I begin writing this book, my mind reflects on the year 2012, in October, in a house in East Stroudsburg, Pennsylvania. At that time, my wife (Darnelle McCullough), my son (Norman J. McCullough Jr.), and I were getting ready to move to Concord (derived from a French word that means "harmony"), North Carolina. Subsequently, the only person we knew in Concord, North Carolina, was my wife's cousin, Sandra Smiling. Mrs. Smiling was very helpful to us and made sure that our new home/apartment was ready for occupation. At that point and time, I knew nothing about Warren C. Coleman. In fact, I never heard the name nor did I have a clue as to who he was. As such, I was on the bottom of the learning curve.

After traveling from East Stroudsburg, Pennsylvania, to Concord, North Carolina, we arrived at our new home and began our new life as Southerners in North Carolina. Having read about the Great Migration North in the early twentieth century, I felt like we were part of a smaller migration of Northerners moving South in the twenty-first century. In other cases, Southerners were moving back home. Due to the cost of living and other factors in the North, many people like us were moving to Charlotte, North Carolina, and other areas in the South, especially as people prepared for their retirement years.

Upon arriving in Concord, North Carolina, it was clear that my retirement years would have to be postponed because I still needed to work in order to purchase a new home and continue to help the community, given my Ivy League education. As a college graduate with a BA from Hunter College and an MA from Teachers College, Columbia University, I knew my work was not complete. At Columbia, I also earned an ABD (all but the dissertation) in 1992. I found Concord, North Carolina, to be a nice, quiet small town where the cost of living was great and where my family and I could live, work, and learn about the awesome history of the town.

John Street United Methodist Church

Prior to thinking about moving South, between 2002 and 2005, I found myself praying at the John Street United Methodist Church in Lower Manhattan. I would go to the church on a regular basis during the week because I was under a tremendous amount of stress, and the church was a few blocks from my office. I was under stress, I later learned, because my former employer, the New York City Housing Authority (NYCHA), was also under a tremendous amount of financial stress. Because I was a deputy director, responsible for fair housing education and related matters, making close to six figures, I was one of the administrative staff (administrative staff analyst) that needed to be expelled by force if necessary. My work performance was not a consideration. After working over ten years at NYCHA and a total of twenty-two years with the City of New York, I earned and I was entitled to my pension. To make the long story short, I was able to retire on my own terms in 2005. In other words, I was able to retire with my full pension minus three years before I became eligible for social security. Retiring early did cause some hardship for me and my family. However, it was evident that my prayers made a difference; and for God's grace,

I will be eternally grateful. Having to retire without my pension would have been a horror.

I later learned that the AME Zion Church (the church that I would join once in North Carolina) was developed/born at the John Street United Methodist Church. I don't believe that this fact is a coincidence. In 2016, I was able to revisit the John Street United Methodist Church, after not seeing it from 2005 when I retired. I was able to speak with one of the members and explain my experience as a person who benefited from praying in the church. I told the person that I was now worshipping at the AME Zion Church in Concord, North Carolina. He directed me to look at a plaque in the church honoring Bishop Varick and others who developed the AME Zion Church while attending the John Street Church. This revisit was important in acknowledging that there was a connection between Price Memorial and the John Street United Methodist Church. Was I given an assignment? I believe so. What specifically the task was was not very clear, but I was certain that God made a way for me. He made a way out of no way. If anyone in the world questions whether there is a God, please tell them to read about my story. It is a story of survival because I was able to retire with my pension. My wife (Darnelle) would also be able to benefit from it because if I passed before her, she would be able to receive my pension until she passed. What an awesome blessing. Anyone going to school and learning about the AME Zion community will know that the John Street United Methodist Church was its place of origination—its place of birth. Why blacks left the John Street United Methodist Church is another story for another author. My point for this book is that in 2005, I did not know anything about the AME Zion Church. I did not know anything about Warren C. Coleman, and I did not know there was a connection among Frederick Douglass, Booker T. Washington, Dr. Joseph C. Price, and Bishop J. W. Hood. And my journey was to fulfill my assignment as a child of God.

Given my experience as a member of the Calvary United Methodist Church–Roselle in East Orange, New Jersey, for over twenty-five years, one of the first task in moving to Concord, North Carolina, was to locate a church.

Selecting a Church

I needed a church for two purposes. One was to continue to worship God, and the other was to locate a space so that I could continue my mentoring service that was incorporated in 2004 at Calvary United Methodist Church–Roselle in East Orange, New Jersey. Further background information about my mentoring services can be gleaned from my first book, *The Dream: A Manual to Facilitate Group Mentoring and Prevent High School Dropouts*,[1] which was published in 2012. After speaking to people at several churches, it was clear to me that Price Memorial AME Zion Church was the best location for me to continue my work as an educator. I also believed that my calling was to touch as many young people as possible in a manner similar to how my family (Gloria McCullough and Mabel and Leona Barzey) and many others touched me. When my mother became ill, my other relatives stepped in to save me from the criminal justice system. They stepped in so that I could fulfill my task as a child of God. I chose Price because when I spoke to one of the members, Mrs. Ella Mae Small, on the phone, I heard voices of some young people in the background. It appeared that Price Memorial was my kind of place. It also had an appropriate space to educate our youth. Again, I will repeat this several times, I knew *nothing* about J. W. Hood, Joseph C. Price, or Warren C. Coleman. I also did not know that Mrs. Small and her husband, the late Allen T. Small, were on the city council and were iconic figures for the town.

Feeling the Hand of God

Clearly, someone was guiding my body to be in the right place at the right time. I felt the same hand at the John Street United Methodist Church, where the Methodist Zion community was born, which was also unknown to me at the time. Before discussing my work at Price Memorial AME Zion Church, I must acknowledge two other people from the area that made a difference for me. One was affectionately known as Bishop Roland Jordan, and the other was Mr. Amos McClorey. Bishop Jordan introduced me to many of the local people like Rev. Donald Anthony, Ms. Wilma Means, and many others. Mr. McClory was the head of the local NAACP, and he provided access to a room where I could begin my mentoring program for no charge. These two men made a great difference in my life. As I began my work in Concord, North Carolina, by teaching eleven students as part of McCullough's Active Mentoring Services (MAMS), I also began to work with Price Memorial to assist them and learn about their massive history. Some of the early students included Nathan Stainback, Joshua Ford, and Tnia Phifer. Coupled with my work at the church, I also began my college teaching career at Rowan-Cabarrus Community College (RCCC) as an adjunct, teaching world civilization, American history, and African-American history. My career at RCCC was a great experience, and I will always remember the hundreds of students that I had a chance to touch from 2013 until. I will also remember Ms. Robin Satterwhite dearly. As one of the leaders in the college, she made an enormous difference to my career. Ms. Satterwhite and others in the college enabled me to teach and influence hundreds of students in Rowan and Cabarrus County, North Carolina. I felt that working with God to touch so many young people was part of my calling.

Meeting Warren C. Coleman

My first encounter with Warren C. Coleman came in 2013 when I learned about a seminar that was being held at the local library on Union Street. At the seminar, with my wife, I observed several members of Price Memorial—Ms. Pearl Asbury, Ms. Willie Jean Boger, and Ms. Eleanor Butler—and fifteen to twenty white people who obviously knew more than I did about this black man who would later begin to saturate my life with his life and times. Knowing what I know now, I am certain that some of the people were from the Barringer family. As I began to learn about Coleman's many activities, one of the first points of information that struck me was the fact that Warren C. Coleman and others built Price Memorial from the ground up. This fact was a major point of movement for me on the learning curve. The next point of movement on the learning curve was reading a book authored by Bernard Davis. I later learned that Mr. Davis was still alive. I met Mr. Davis, and he was gracious enough to give me a private tour of the Warren C. Coleman Estate. My mind started to swell, growing bigger by the hour. How come people did not know about this man (Coleman)? And if they did, why wasn't his story being publicized to the world?

I later learned that Mr. Coleman had a store on Union Street and that he built a seventeen-acre cemetery on Cabarrus Avenue, near the Martin Luther King roundabout. Moreover, I learned that he built an extensive mill (196,000 sq. ft., later modified after his death), and he also built close to one hundred homes near the mill (and various other parts of Concord) so that his workers could have a place to live. Another major thesis of this book is that Coleman and his supporters were planning to build a mill town so that people could satisfy all their needs—from church, food, work, etc. After reading several books, newspaper articles, and various other documents, it became very clear to me that Mr. Coleman was known to some people; but clearly, he was unknown to most people in America. In addition, although many of the documents outlined his background living in a Confederate world, the connection between his black world and white world was not fully flushed out. Given my education, overall work experience, and government experience working for the City of New York and the federal government for seven years, it became evident that my job or raison d'être was to gather as much information as possible to share Coleman's story for the world to see.

As indicated in the Bible at Matthew 5:14–16,

> Ye are the light of the world. A city that is set on a hill cannot be hid. Neither do men light a candle and put it under a bushel, but on a candle stick and it giveth light unto all that are in the house. Let your light so shine before men, that they may see your good works, and glorify your Father which is in heaven.

Coleman and the 100 Black Men of America Inc.

Moreover, as a member of the 100 Black Men Inc. in New York City (it was incorporated in 1963) since 1979 until 2006, which was the founding chapter, I am certain that Coleman would have qualified as a member, sponsored by a person like myself. Prior to the development of the Eagle Academy, the 100 Black Men Inc. of New York City had a mentoring program for high school seniors. The mentoring program, starting in the late 1980s and into the 1990s, was initiated by Dr. Roscoe C. Brown. He was my mentor, and I learned the basics of group mentoring from him. After Dr. Brown retired from the organization, myself, Fermin Archer, Rudy Clause, Rudy Coombs, Mark Fant, Esq., Ozzie Fletcher, Leslie Wyche, and many others agreed to continue to provide mentors for each young person receiving a scholarship from the organization. All these men were doers. I was the chair of the mentoring committee. We were also able to obtain corporate sponsors like New York BlueCross BlueShield (headed by Dr. Michael Stocker), Metropolitan Life Insurance, the New York Stock Exchange, Chase Manhattan Bank, and many others. Moreover, due to the mentoring program sponsored by the 100 Black Men Inc., the members were able to meet people like Johnnie Cochran, Rudy Crew (president of Medgar Evers College in Brooklyn), and Oprah Winfrey. After being honored at the annual gala, decided to give $100,000 in scholarship money for future recipients. In addition, during this same period, members of the Metropolitan Museum of Art agreed to have several members of the organization become members of the advisory committee. Based on this activity, the organization decided to open and develop an Eagle Academy under the jurisdiction of the New York Board of Education in the Bronx. Under the leadership of David Banks, Esq., and many others, there are Eagle Academies in all five boroughs and in Newark, New Jersey. On my Facebook page, I have observed dozens of young people wearing Eagle apparel and enjoying the legacy and work of hundreds of men in New York City and beyond.

If Coleman had lived beyond 1904, W. E. B. Du Bois would have considered him a member of the talented tenth.[2] We often say that money is not everything, but without it, it is difficult to do many positive things. The 100 Black Men Inc., located in most cities throughout the USA, is an organization that I served for over twenty-five years. I served for over twelve years on the board of directors. It is an organization for black professional men like Coleman, enabling them to have comradery, to mentor young people, and to give back to the community in ways that would not be possible to do by themselves as individuals.

Professionals, both black and white, oftentimes provide mentoring for people in at-risk environments. If one thinks about it, Coleman was offering training/mentoring to hundreds of men and women who were locked out of industrial occupations in various parts of the South. Lest we forget those who paved a way for people like me and other African-Americans living in the South and later in the North.

Rationale for the Book

Why was this book about Warren C. Coleman written? This book was written because, as indicated previously, people in the city of Concord, the state of North Carolina, the United States of America, and others around the world must know that black men and women in America (some former slaves) made a difference and will continue to make a difference. As one great author would say, "And still we rise."[3]

In addition, the evidence that will be presented shows that Coleman was the richest black man in America in 1900. Another reason for writing this book is an attempt to heal the great divide that remains in this country. A divide that some of our enemies will use to hurt us, given our experience in 2016. Having the Russians interfere with our election should be a major wake-up call. As Americans, both white and nonwhite, we must do everything in our power to remain together. Remaining together, unfortunately, may not be in the interest of some Americans. This book will demonstrate that we are together whether we like it or not. We have a common heritage.

This book will also review the life of Warren C. Coleman as a young man from a black person's perspective. Many people have written about Mr. Coleman, but none has written an entire book about him exclusively from the perspective of the Zion community and the viewpoint of the African-American experience. This book, unlike most, will also attempt to integrate the Colemans with the Barringers. I am talking about the Coleman/Barringer family. What did Coleman do as a chattel slave in America? Did he have a master? He was born in 1849, a few years before the beginning of the Civil War. What do we know about his father, mother, brothers, sisters, etc.? Like so many other great leaders in America—such as Frederick Douglass, Booker T. Washington, and many others—Coleman was fathered by a white male: Rufus Barringer.

Coleman's beginning, like so many others, was and continues to be an American story. The story of some white men fighting for slavery and fathering black children, but in some cases, not wanting anyone to know was common. In other cases, children did know who their fathers were. Some, like Coleman, knew who their fathers were; and according to the record, his father made a positive difference in his early life. Coleman's father, Rufus Barringer, was a member of the Southern gentry; and the story of Coleman's father will also be outlined. Many of his family members were attorneys, including all his (Barringer's) brothers. Rufus Barringer rose to become a general in the Confederate Army. Prior to the Civil War, Rufus was the mayor of Concord for three years. Like Coleman, the life and times of General Barringer is known by some, but too many are not aware of his life or his times. In the spirit of the Methodist church, one being on the wrong side of history does not mean that his story should not be told. General Barringer, according to the record, accepted his black sons; but he did not advertise it to the world. The town of Concord, as is the case with Thomas Jefferson's black children, knew that some people looked like one another. Whether he (Barringer) told everyone about his two black sons, especially after he was married to three different white women, is another matter. According to S. Barringer, "Rufus would not have been allowed to court Eugenia had her father known of Rufus's two illegitimate mulatto sons ... Somehow, his political adversaries and the press never learned of the relationship until just after his passing."[4]

Giving to Others

Given Coleman's life and times, he decided, taking into consideration his circumstance, to become an entrepreneur; however, his work in serving as a philanthropist in the community must not be overlooked. Coleman, as the record will show, was a wealthy man compared to the average black man after the Civil War. Relatively speaking, Coleman was a billionaire. Because of his wealth, Mr. Coleman was able to build/ finance a seventeen-acre cemetery, the Old Camp Ground Cemetery

(OCGC), where eighteen veterans and others were buried. This was because blacks could not be buried in white cemeteries in the South prior to the 1960s. Coleman and Mr. Frank Logan (educator in Concord for over forty years) are also buried in this historic location (see newspaper by Gail Smith-Arrants, dated May 3, 2001). Mr. Coleman gave money to churches, colleges, and many other entities where he saw the need to assist the black community. The book will also review his relationship with the AME Zion Church and, more specifically, include the Zion Hill AME Zion Church and Price Memorial AME Zion Church seen in chapter 5. Several photos and documents of his life and times will also be included. Moreover, unknown to many people, the record will show that Coleman also had several imported horses and had a relationship with Booker T. Washington. On a preliminary basis, according to Washington in his book *Up from Slavery*,[5] Coleman was with him when he made his famous speech at the 1895 Atlanta Exposition.

A Significant Transition in Black Leadership

This book will explore the Coleman-Washington relationship and explore the idea that Coleman received many of his ideas regarding the mill from the time that he spent with Washington in 1895. What is the significance of 1895? If one looks at the stone in front of Price Memorial, one will see that it says that the church was built in 1895, the same year that Mr. Coleman and Mr. Washington were in Atlanta, Georgia, for the great Atlanta Exposition. Eighteen ninety-five is also the year that the leader of black America, Frederick Douglass, passed away and blacks in America were looking for another leader. Due to the passing of Dr. Joseph C. Price in 1893 (Price was being prepared to be the leader by many), the leadership mantle fell to Booker T. Washington. In the book by Krieger, we see that even though Coleman never met Douglass, Douglass had a feeling about a black textile mill: "Frederick Douglass—the Negro Orator and Journalist, advocated the development of a black owned cotton mill."[6]

Another important consideration in discussing the mill is to understand that the mill was not a just a textile mill, as conceived by Coleman. According to the incorporation papers and in a book written by Krieger, "The Articles of Incorporation authorized the company to issue five hundred, one hundred dollar shares ... Authorization was given to produce textile yarn cloth, and sell and convey real estate ... not to exceed one thousand acres and build upon and improve lease and rent real estate."[7]

How and why did Coleman pass away? This book will discuss Coleman's passing and the fact that Mr. Coleman passed away in his home on Cabarrus Avenue (formerly Depot Street) and Church Street. This book and the many other events that will be held to celebrate, including an annual street fair, will continue the legacy of this great hidden figure in American history. Coleman was not only a great African-American, he was also a great American who worked to service his community—both white and black.

Previous Acknowledgments and Celebration

During my time working with Price Memorial (from 2013), I learned that others, on or about 2001, like myself began to understand the enormous legacy of Mr. Coleman. People like myself, from the North/South, decided to apply for the erection of the North Carolina State Highway Marker next to the mill on Route 601 in 2001.[8] I will discuss the people involved and make note of their efforts to begin the process of acknowledging this great man for the world to see. Unlike Mr. Cannon and Mr. Odell (both great manufacturers from Concord who also built mills), Mr. Coleman, because of his color and his racial and economic status, has not been given the same appropriate accolades and material investment for the world to see. Hopefully the publication of this book, coupled with Coleman's work, will continue to put the light on a candlestick. In early 2015, having moved up the learning curve, I decided with others to make every attempt to gain access to the mill. With the assistance of the current owner (Mr. Bill Bryant), members of the church, and many others (like Mr. Dennis Rowe and Mr. Thomas Dixon), we were able to acquire a bus and have three trips around the Coleman Estate (church, location of his home [down Cabarrus, formerly known as Depot Street where Zion Hill was located] the mill, and the cemetery and return) in 2015. Rev. Johnny McClure of Price Memorial was a major supporter. The experience around the mill and inside the mill was awesome. To think that a former chattel slave born in America, with the assistance of others, could build such a structure (now 196,000 sq. ft.) was mind-bending.

This mill, if one is aware of the history of Egypt/Kemet, could be considered a pyramid in America. As we move into the future, it is my prayer that the legacy of this great man can be reinforced and given the necessary resources to ensure that future generations, both white and black, can understand what it takes to overcome historical adversities in America and other parts of the world. We will continue to overcome and understand that it is not where you begin but where you are going.

I never knew my biological father (John Williams). I knew my stepfather (Andrew McCullough), who was not a role model by any means. Warren C. Coleman was a role model. He was a role model for all Americans seeking to understand that one can't control who your parents are and one can't control where and how much money you have when you are born, but one can control what you do with your life—in spite of the many obstacles you may face. Looking at the life and times of Warren C. Coleman, one can see a clear example of another former American slave rising above and beyond, making a difference for us all.

In concluding this chapter, Price Memorial and the City of Concord have agreed to hold an annual street fair on Union Street to celebrate Coleman. As a fundraiser for the church (Price Memorial), the proceeds will continue the work started by Coleman and many others. Having this activity, coupled with other events that may develop, will ensure that the Coleman legacy and his life and times will continue over the years for future generations to share.

Chapter Two

Warren C. Coleman's Early Life and Slavery

What, to the American slave is the 4th of July?
I answer, a day that reveals to him, more than
all other days in the year, the gross injustice
cruelty to which he is a constant victim,
—Frederick Douglass

Birth of an American Entrepreneur

The record indicates that Coleman was born an illegitimate son of Rufus Barringer and a slave, Roxana Coleman (Mr. Burgess says her name was Roxie). Coleman was born on the twenty-eighth day of March 1849. Regarding the early life of Concord (1838), Clarence E. Horton Jr. said, "Tax list shows 'taxable' in Concord as 46 white males and 29 African-American males."[9] It appears that because Coleman lived an ordinary life prior to his development as a manufacturer, there is very little known knowledge about his boyhood, except that he worked for the Confederacy as a teenager during the Civil War. He was a slave and worked accordingly. If we look at his birth in 1849, by 1861, he was twelve years old. And by the end of the war in 1865, he was sixteen years old. Given this early part of his life, his options to do something other than to work for the Confederacy were limited.

Moreover, blacks could not carry firearms. As noted by Blight, we have the case of John Brown's raid on Harpers Ferry and how Douglass was becoming more and more violence prone and willing to use guns: "If speech could end slavery, Douglass said it would have been done long ago. He demanded an 'anti-slavery Government' but the political system seemed to offer only 'can't' and he was sick of it. Hence, the ballot is needed, and if this will not be heard and heeded, then the bullet."[10] This refrain sounds like Malcolm X, who also spoke about the ballot or the bullet. Prior to the Civil War, the number of free blacks was significant according to Gates: "So what do the actual numbers of black slave owners and their slaves tell us? In 1830 about 13.7 percent (319,599) of the black population was free. Of these free Negroes, 3,776 owned 12,209 slaves, out of a total of 2,009,043 owned in the entire United States. So the number of slaves owned by black people overall was quite small in comparison with the number of slaves owned by white people."[11]

Another source indicates that in North Carolina, the number of slaves from 1820 to 1820 rose from 206,017 to 331,059. This same source also makes the point that some African-Americans also owned slaves.3 Why, is the question. According to Gates in *100 Amazing Facts about the Negro*, in 1830, about 33,776 free blacks owned 12,907 slaves. Some wanted, if they could, to protect friends or relatives; but others were interested in the financial benefits. The record also indicates that two states had more slaves than whites (South Carolina and Mississippi), but in North Carolina, we see that a third of all people were slaves, with a very small free black population. Hines also makes that point that white men having children with black slaves was common, and the most infamous was Thomas Jefferson and Sally Hemings. Jefferson started having children with Hemings when she was fourteen. Like the case of Roxana Coleman, the issue of statutory rape was not applicable at the time. How America will satisfy the abuse of this practice over three hundred years is one where black men will always remember how their wives, sisters, and daughters were treated as part of the American story, when America was "great."

Female Slaves

As I told many people about my book, some said some attention should be paid to the female slaves who were oftentimes ignored. Women like Roxana Coleman, Jane Coleman, Sally Hemings, and many others were ignored and never discussed in any great detail. For Roxana and Jane (Coleman's wife), there is just very little record to look at. This fact is unfortunate and another clear example of lost history. We also know that Roxana followed an older slave around to learn respect, obedience, and diligence. However, in the case of Sally Hemings, we see that Sally was born in 1773 and died in 1835, fourteen years before Coleman was born. Like Roxana, the history of Sally is not extensive, especially at a young age; but because she belonged to the president, we know a little more. Her father was John Wayles, and her mother was Elizabeth Hemings, a slave. If her father were a slave and her mother was free, Sally would have been free. The record is clear that Sally had six children with Jefferson. Two of her sisters also bore children with white men. All their children were slaves even though their fathers were free. Why this system was established is the subject of review for another writer (see Annette Gordon-Reed's "Did Sally Hemings and Thomas Jefferson Love Each Other?"). In the case of Roxana, the evidence indicates that Rufus had a love relationship with his neighbor's slave. Ms. Reed makes this point regarding Sally and Jefferson: "Many white men have acted (and do act) selfishly and cowardly in their relationship with black women. This does not mean that none of these men had (or have) feelings that we would not recognize as a form of love."[12] Or is it a form of lust that may be interpreted as love? It is very complicated for my brain; but when one really thinks about it, loving a person, another human being, who merits the status of a slave is not someone you love. In spite of the evidence presented by Ms. Gordon-Reed in 1997, there are many who don't want to believe that the president could have had sex with a light-skinned black slave. "Although Sally Hemings lived at Monticello for 36 years, there is not a scintilla of proof of any intimate conduct between her and Jefferson, or any demonstrations of affection or commerce of any kind ... Inferences that Jefferson had intercourse merely because he was the master and Hemings was a slave may not be drawn without some proof of a physical relationship."[13] What else do we need—a photo? Even that would not be enough for some.

The Number of Slaves in America

Slavery in America is one that we, as a country, have not come to grips with in any real form. From 1964 to 1968, it can be said that the reconciliation period began for blacks when they were given their true freedom from Jim Crow and the like. From 1968 to 2019, several attempts have been made to address this enormous stain on the country. Recently, my wife and I were talking about how blacks have been affected by slavery in America. We noted that whites, in order to have full compliance, attempted to strip African-Americans of everything from them to conform to the idea of chattel or property. Everything included language, manner of speech, history, diet, and many other attributes that would mean that the slave masters were not dealing with human beings, which puts American slavery in the realm not seen anywhere else in the world at any other time. Everything was stripped except music. Music is what African-Americans and other blacks in the world have in common. It could be jazz music from the diaspora or beats related to the drum. After four hundred years of inhabitation in America, it is clear that black people throughout the world have felt that same connection. Whether we are talking about music from Cuba, Brazil, the Caribbean, or the southern or northern parts of America, we can feel the beat. I am sure that Roxana, her two sons, and her husband could also feel the beat. I am certain that Warren C. Coleman could also feel the beat, which is why the assimilation process for blacks becomes very difficult in white America. Or is that whites will have to assimilate with blacks? The picture in front of this book speaks for itself, with respect to Coleman's connection to the black community. We are connected to the motherland of Africa through the music, just like how other Americans are connected to St. Patrick's or Columbus Day. It is part of their DNA.

As we discuss the number of slaves in America, it must be understood that most slaves were sent to South America or the Caribbean (10.7 million in total, but only 388,000 landed in America, as indicated by

Louis Gates in his *100 Amazing Facts about the Negro*). Brazil alone received 4.8 million; and it appears, without additional proof, that the Coleman farm had three slaves: Roxana and her two sons, Thomas and Warren. It should be noted that when Roxana got married to John Young, he became another slave on the farm. However, the record indicates that Rufus's father, Paul, had as many as fifteen slaves but later decided that slavery was not appropriate. These facts mean that slavery was in the neighborhood for some time. Mostly in the South, having numerous slaves was common in states like South Carolina, Georgia, Louisiana, North Carolina, and other Southern States. It should be understood that most of the US presidents owned slaves, including George Washington, James Madison, Andrew Jackson, Martin Van Buren, John Tyler, James Polk, Zachary Taylor, Ulysses Grant (through his wife), and many others like Benjamin Franklin. People like William Rufus King, Stephen Duncan, Joseph Hayes Acklen, Robert Francis Allston, Joseph Blake, and John Burnside had hundreds of slaves on various plantations. How America overcomes this legacy of slavery and its remnants remains to be seen. Warren C. Coleman was a part of this legacy, and his various deeds must be viewed in this context. Most slaves were not able to overcome this legacy or make something of themselves. However, the norm was to succumb to the horrors of the slave lifestyle or run away to the North or die in the process. After leaving the Coleman farm in 1870, Warren left Concord and went to Alabama to ascertain what was happening in Tuskegee. Coleman's wife, Jane, was from Alabama.

In 1973, for one or two years, Coleman attended Howard University. He was twenty-four years old. It is important to note that in his possession, Coleman had a written recommendation from Bishop J. W. Hood. At the time that Coleman attended Howard, we see another famous African-American, T. Thomas Fortune. The connection between Mr. Fortune and Mr. Coleman will be discussed further in the book. Another famous person attending around the same time was John C. Dancy. After returning from Washington, DC, Coleman began his career as a businessman by continuing to operate a store on Union Street. Today, there is a small marker indicating where his store was located, across from the Old Court House. In 1876, twenty-seven years after his birth, Mr. Coleman and three trustees from Zion Hill

AME Zion Church purchased seventeen acres to enable blacks to be buried in a dignified manner in a dignified place, later known as the Old Camp Ground Cemetery (OCGC). Over the years, the cemetery was able to hold the remains of over two hundred people, including eighteen veterans. In the book by Rouse, we see that the people included in the sale were Warren C. Coleman, Richard McCree, John Young, and Ephraim Means of Zion Hill Church. They paid a total of $595 for seventeen acres, split into two equal payments.[14] In his book, Mr. Rouse does very little or nothing to connect Coleman to his Coleman or Barringer family.

People like Mr. Coleman, his wife (Jane Coleman), Emily Bowman-Reynolds Alexander, Jacob "Jake" Wallace, Dr. William Charles W. C. Baucum, Rev. Frank Logan, and many others too numerous to mention are buried at the OCGC. It appears that people continued to be buried at the cemetery until the 1960s, which would make sense given the federal legislation ending the era of Jim Crow and the like. I learned from nearby neighbors that the pavement currently seen on the entrance was completed about seventeen years ago, and the Cannon Mills Foundation put up the archway in the front, at the entrance on Cabarrus Avenue. It appears that the Cannon Foundation, although limited, has made various attempts to support black landmarks; but without the support of the entire town, their efforts will not have long-term success. Prior to the archway, there was only a dirt road and a post with some chains to help prevent intruders from driving in.

In the 1880s, Coleman operated a store that featured a barbershop; and he also sold cake, candy, canned goods, tar, etc. In addition, according to a newspaper article titled "Cabarrus Neighbor" by Helen Arthur,[15] "Even as a child, young Warren was interested in commerce, Rankin's report says, he sold live rabbits for a nickel apiece and saved those nickels. Later he bought a horse, then sold it for a horse and a wagon." In the same newspaper, we see that he was before his time. It said, "As a young man, Coleman brought a half-acre of land on Church Street for $600.00." Moreover, Ms. Arthur states that "people bought his black walnuts, chestnuts, fresh cakes and candies, coffee and tea, [sic] canned goods 'New Orleans Black Strap Molasses' and his nickel rabbits and partridges and dipped axle grease from a tar pit behind the store at 15 cents a pint."[16] It should also be noted that in 2001, a plaque was placed on the location where Coleman operated his store. We also see that he advertised houses for rent. However, in 1885, his store burned to the ground; but he was able to recover and acquire many other properties. As a young black man living in the Jim Crow South, having his store burn was something that happened to both whites and blacks. The record, as noted in the *North-Carolina Gazette* on September 26, 1885, indicates that there is a letter from Mr. J. H. Williamson that says, "By a disastrous fire in the town last Saturday Night ... Mr. Warren C. Coleman suffered a least $5,000. This is the third time that Mr. Coleman has been burned out within five years without insurance."[17] Why would a man have to suffer so many fires? Was his color a consideration? We must remember that the late 1800s was a period of severe racial hatred, as I will discuss further in the book.

Moreover, a number of whites fought to challenge Coleman's acquisition of land, and one of these was Mr. Hartshell, and he litigated some of these issues in court. Coleman did not prevail. As such, having so much success may have been a problem for some people. I later learned that once the mill was built, Coleman moved his store to Depot Avenue (currently known as Cabarrus Avenue), near Scotia College. In the late 1880s, Coleman was able to sell a plot of land to Mr. Odell for a major profit. According to some, "his generosity became legendary among North Carolina Negroes. He served as Chief Commissioner for the North Carolina Negro Exhibit at the Cotton States and International Exposition in Atlanta."[18]

In another source drafted by Mr. Bernard Davis, we see that Coleman was a man who wanted to service the needs of the people of Concord and beyond. It says, "From the very start, Mr. Coleman seemed to have an uncanny business sense for what was most needed by people in the area. He realized early on that rabbits needed by a farmer to feed his family could be traded for an idle plow and the plow traded for a lamp oil and so on and so on."[19]

Chapter Three

Warren C. Coleman's Family and Confederate Background

North Carolina was going to hell but I am going with her.
—Rufus Barringer

Warren C. Barringer

Given his birth to Rufus C. Barringer and Roxana Coleman, Coleman was like many other slaves whose father was a white male and whose mother was a black female slave. A picture of Roxana can be seen in a newly published book by Sheridan R. Barringer.[20] Given different normal circumstances, Warren's name should be Warren Clay Barringer. In my own case, my true name should be Norman Williams, but my mother did not want me to know about Mr. Williams. I did not learn specifically until I moved with my relatives at the age of sixteen, and they gave me the news that my biological father was an older man when I was born.

The record also indicates that General Barringer had another older son with Roxana. Barringer's older son with Roxana was known as Thomas. Very little is known about Thomas. The record indicates that Thomas was born on June 2, 1845, which means he was four years older than Warren. In the S. Barringer book, we see that Thomas, in an 1870 census, was living in a boarding house in Raleigh, North Carolina. The record also shows that Thomas married three times and had two children.[21] As such, on the Roxana Coleman side of the family, we know that she also had three children with another man, John Young. Subsequently, Roxana had a total of six children. Two with General Barringer, three with Mr. John Young, and another with Joseph Smith. The number of children Roxana had remains unclear, but what is clear was that Warren was exceptional. "Cabarrus County Records reveal that Coleman entered the mercantile business in Concord as early as December of the year 1872."[22]

Rufus Barringer—Mayor and Reluctant Warrior

The record indicates that Rufus Barringer, prior to becoming a general, went to NC State University and practiced law. He also became a member of the lower house of the state legislature before the war, starting in 1848, a year before the birth of Coleman. On the Barringer side of the family, first there was Coleman's father (Rufus Barringer), his three wives, and his children (Anna Morrison, Paul Barringer, Rufus Jr., and Osmond).

According to several sources, in a brief outline, one notes that Rufus Barringer did not want to secede from the Union but later agreed with his state and decided to join the Confederate Army. After rising through the ranks and becoming a brigadier general, Rufus fought in the battles of Chancellorsville, Second Manassas, Antietam (or Sharpsburg), Fredericksburg Dinwiddie (resulting in a Union victory), and others. General Barringer's older brother was Victor Clay Barringer. Today we can see a marker placed on Union Street (on the grounds of Cannon Library in Concord) where President Jefferson Davis spent time at his (Victor's) home. While Daniel M. Barringer, Rufus's oldest brother, served in Congress with President Lincoln from 1844 to 1849.[23]

During this same time period (1845 and 1849), General Barringer made it possible to have two children with a slave, Roxana, and at the same time travel to various parts of the country, as noted in the new book by Sheridan Barringer: "Despite these obligations, Rufus found time to travel north for five weeks during May and June of 1946. He visited Boston, Saratoga Springs in New York and Washington."[24]

Barringer's Love Affair with Roxana

Before getting married to several white women, General Barringer, as noted previously, had two children with Roxana. Sheridan Barringer states in his book, published in 2016, that General Barringer had a love affair with a slave living with his neighbor, Daniel Coleman.[25] Prior to seeing this information in the Barringer book, I surmised that Rufus and Roxana were in love. The information in Barringer's book substantiated the point, especially when it is clear that the relationship lasted for four years. There is additional support for the love relationship when S. Barringer states, "The connection between Rufus and Roxana, however, was supported by Holland Thompson, who knew Rufus Barringer and served as the superintendent of Concord's public schools during the 1890's ... He was born a slave and his reputed father was a white man, afterward distinguished by military and financial ability, who is said to have assisted the boy."[26]

Clearly there is evidence that indicates that Rufus assisted Warren, but not when he needed it most. Of course, Rufus passed in 1895, a year before Warren announced that he was going to open a mill in Concord. Rufus could have reached out and indicate that he would offer his services beforehand. He could have made a difference in Coleman's life. Rufus could have also spoken to his son Paul and conveyed to him that Warren was an honorable man who deserved his help. This could have been done except for one thing—slavery. Slavery has caused a lot of damage in America. Yes, many people were able to get rich due to cotton and the like. However, the cost in human misery is immeasurable, and we are still dealing with it today. The cost in terms of wasted human resources is still being felt, especially when you think about the financial resources expended every year on people who are unable to take care of themselves due to the legacy of slavery and Jim Crow. Those incarcerated in our criminal justice system (the largest in the world) would instead be able to pay taxes and contribute to the overall society. Moreover, imagine the United States without slavery and Jim Crow; the cost of having both systems does not outweigh the saving and cultural benefits of having neither. A conversation between General Barringer and Roxana over a four-year period may have gone as follows:

> BARRINGER. You are a slave, and I am an attorney, but I still want to be with you.

> ROXANA COLEMAN. Yes, I know, and Thomas and Warren are your children. What are your plans?

> BARRINGER. I am not sure. Go to sleep.

Prior to fighting in the war, there is written proof that Rufus Barringer was the mayor of Concord from 1857 to 1859. According to Kathryn L. Bridges and Eugenia Lore, Daniel Coleman was mayor from 1859 to 1860 and in 1863. The record also shows that Daniel Coleman (William Coleman's father) was a commissioner in 1845 and from 1853 to 1856. Clearly, prior to the Civil War, the Colemans and Barringers were in control of Concord in more ways than one. It is also observed that many of the family members on the Coleman side and the Barringer side were attorneys.[27] It should also be understood that honoring Warren is also honoring his family, both direct and extended. Just because one portion is white and another is black should not separate their efforts to make a positive impact on the City of Concord and the United States of America.

General Barringer

General Barringer is well-known due to the fact that he was the first Confederate general to meet President Lincoln after he was captured and placed in a Union prison. President Lincoln was interested in meeting General Barringer because he was under the impression that General Rufus Barringer was his older brother, Daniel. General Barringer was also known as the commander of the North Carolina Cavalry Brigade, and many of its battles are well documented. For example, in an article by Wilford Kale in the *Daily Press* (dated December 3, 2018), we see that his brigade was very active: "If you don't recognize the name of Rufus Barringer that is not surprising even for civil war buffs, but the Carolina Brigade may be a different story. That Confederate Unit participated in more than 160 engagements of various types from skirmishes to major battles from 1861–1865."8 General Barringer's capture toward the end of the war was noted by Helen Arthur-Cornett: "By war's end, he had risen to general and was an honored prisoner of war, captured by Yankees wearing Confederate uniforms."[28] Also see a copy of the article dated June 17, 2021.

General Barringer was married three times due to illness and later death. First, he was married to Eugenia Morrison. He later married Rosallie Chunn. And last, General Barringer married Margaret Taylor Long. Due to his marriage to Eugenia, General Barringer was also related to General Stonewall Jackson and General D. H. Hill. Her sisters were married to these two men. Clearly, if the South had won the war, all these people would have been on top of the economic order in the new nation and blacks would have remained on the bottom or the institution of slavery would have existed for many years. Nevertheless, as God would have it, like Dr. Joseph C. Price who became the president of Livingstone College, Eugenia's father became the president of Davidson College. All these institutions may not have existed without the sacrifices of these great men. Nonetheless, the facts are that the ancestors of these great institutions have family connections that some may want to ignore, but no one can deny.

According to S. Barringer, Rufus held a distinction no other Confederate general was able to say. He said, "General Barringer had been captured in the last week of the war, the first general officer taken to the massive Union base at City Point, nine miles northeast of Petersburg. Barringer was also the first Confederate general to meet President Abraham Lincoln, who visited City Point after his tour to meet President Abraham Lincoln, who visited City Point after his tour of fallen Richmond."[29] Before he was captured, however, his neighbor, William Coleman, played a major role in Concord in 1861 when a flag was presented to the Cabarrus Rangers. As noted by S. Barringer, "William Coleman, who would become the state's attorney general in 1868, gave a speech in which he told the assembled men of Company F of the responsibility resting upon them in sustaining that flag."[30]

After the Civil War, General Barringer became a Republican; and in 1880, he supported black suffrage. Moreover, General Barringer could be considered a liberal after the war. It is noted that "he also served on the Board of Trustees of Biddle University, a black school founded by the Presbyterian Church in 1867, located on the outskirts of Charlotte."[31] Its name was later changed to Johnson C. Smith. In another document, it is clear that General Barringer was viewed as a traitor at one point: "Moving to Charlotte during the post war period, he became a 'Radical' Republican and strongly supported Reconstruction, especially James Longstreet, labeled them as 'lepers' in their own community."[32] These negative sentiments were asserted even though Barringer was wounded three times during the Civil War. However, Barringer later switched to the Democratic Party and became successful and later died of stomach cancer in 1895—the same year that Coleman was building Price Temple and returning from the 1895 Atlanta Exposition. What would have happened if Barringer had decided to reach out and help his son before he died? Again we see that race is holding us back as a society. The evidence is clear. If Rufus had helped his son, like other whites helping their sons (both white and black), our society would be changed in very short order.

Coleman's Experience During and After the War

How was Coleman treated before and after the war? In another article by Marvin Krieger, he states, "He [Rufus Barringer] provided inspiration and financial assistance to Coleman's early business ventures and his establishment of a cotton mill."[33] In another article authored by Ricky Riley in *Atlanta Black Star*—"Six Things You Should Know about Warren C. Coleman"—Riley states, "When the mill opened, Coleman hired 300 people to work in his business … From 1901–1904, the mill operated without a hitch."[34] We also see that Warren's master also played a role: "After post-Civil War emancipation, Warren Coleman was bound to Cabarrus Counter Planter-Lawyer, William M. Coleman, the man who provided Warren with an informal education."[35] Why wasn't Coleman given his freedom until 1870? The answer is related to his age. In 1865, Coleman was only sixteen years old. I am certain that Warren must have received much of his legal training during this time under the supervision of his master. The overall documentation shows that Warren was helped by his white family members during the early part of his real estate career. As a black man born in America, I must say that white people have helped me in many ways. There is one person I remember clearly. His name was Mr. Miller, and he was a teacher at Charles Sumner Junior High School on the Lower East Side. After I took a standardized reading test, Mr. Miller observed that I had a ninth-grade reading score even though I was in the seventh grade. He made a special effort to make sure I was in the appropriate class, given the classes were assigned according to reading ability. I went from 7–19 to 9–5.

Moreover, with the assistance of whites, we see that Coleman opened a business: "His first business was a combination of a barbershop and candy store. With financial help from his father, the young businessman purchased land in the African-American community which eventually became know as 'Coleburg and Logan neighborhood.'"[36] The area behind Scotia College was known as Coleburg prior to Logan, named after Rev. Frank Logan. Why the area was called Coleburg is not known. It could be because of the Coleman family. After looking at all the evidence on file and understanding that most of the Coleman and Barringer men were attorneys, it appears to me that the area was called Coleburg due to the influence of the Coleman/Kuhlman family. The name was Americanized after the arrival of Nicholas Kuhlman/ Coleman in America as of 1764.

Black Confederates

Given all the support given by his white family, one may begin to ask, Was Coleman a Confederate? Did he believe in the enslavement of black people? Why didn't he run away like so many other slaves? One may also ask whether he benefited from his status and decided to live in the South as a rich man or go North (like Frederick Douglass) and live his life as a poor man. All these questions are important. However, based on the facts, it is clear that Coleman moving away from the Coleman farm would have been very risky for a teenager who was under eighteen years old at the end of the Civil War. The historical evidence indicates that blacks were utilized in the Confederacy for many purposes. Coleman was one among thousands of unknown former slaves who were forced to support the South during the Civil War. Were they volunteers, or were they forced to fight or work? In an article entitled "Black Confederates" by Sam Smith in the American Battlefield Trust, he states, "Some black Southerners aided the Confederacy. Most of these were forced to accompany their masters or were forced to toil behind the battle lines. Black men were not legally allowed to serve as combat soldiers in the Confederate Army, they were cooks, teamster and manual laborers."[37] However, given the history of slavery in the South, it is clear that if you had a small amount of black blood, you were considered to be black and treated accordingly and not allowed to fight. However, in the Hines book, it is noted that some blacks volunteered to fight but were, for the most part, rejected unless for menial labor.[38]

However, the literature indicates that a small number of blacks may have illegally fought for the Confederacy; people like Robert Stover and others who served as teamsters appear to be the norm. On the other hand, William Ellison was a black slave who decided to later own slaves and support the Confederacy. Why he did so is a mystery to me. In the case of Coleman, it appears that he was a teenager; and because he knew who his father was, he may have felt some allegiance (not having gone to Howard University yet and not having received some higher education). As such, it is also clear that when Coleman was released from bondage from Mr. William M. Coleman in 1870, Warren focused, having been immersed in the legal field, on the needs of African-Americans in need of assistance and left the legacy of the Confederacy in the dustbin of history. There is no evidence that Coleman ever believed that African-Americans should be enslaved or subjected to the rule of white people.

America's Biracial Legacy

Some people, I am certain, would look at Coleman and say that he benefited from white privilege. Yes, his father was white, and his mother was black. If his father were a slave and his mother were free, he would be free. It is weird and horrid, like so much of American slavery—the peculiar institution. Given close to 250 years of chattel slavery, black women were at the mercy of white men. In regard to reparations, how does America pay for this injustice to an entire people from the continent of Africa for close to 250 years of bondage and chattel? As an African-American whose family legacy was first in the Caribbean, my mind continues to be blown by the accomplishment of many of these Southern men and women despite the legacy of chattel slavery. What makes their accomplishments so phenomenal is the fact that these people were treated as property. What other group of people in the world have suffered in a similar manner? My mind goes primarily to the people of ancient Egypt, but even they did not lose their identities or have their women raped on a regular basis. And as in the case of Coleman, some might offer assistance to their children, if men acknowledged their behavior. The most infamous family with regard to racial and sexual injustice that's currently known is the family of President Thomas Jefferson and the slave Sally Hemings. Did he love her? The answer may be yes, but there are many in the country who can't stand the thought of blacks and whites having true love prior to 1865. Our most recent president, Barack Obama, was the product of an interracial marriage. When are we going to admit that America is becoming an interracial society because human beings are human beings? No level of hate can change this fact. As time moves on, the country will come to grips with this fact and change accordingly. I pray to God.

According to the census, the number of people labeled as biracial or others is 2.7 percent during 2018. The total number of people was 327,167,434. The number of nonwhites was 40 (including biracial), and it is projected that both numbers will increase by 2040 or beyond and that nonwhites will outnumber the number of whites. In other words, the majority will become the minority. Accordingly, some people are losing their minds with the prospects of being in the minority. However, this fact may not change things. Looking at South Africa, where the whites are in the minority, the whites still own most of the wealth. Warren C. Coleman was a product of this early phenomenon in our country.

In the Coleman/Barringer family, we are informed that it was obvious that Warren was Rufus's child. Unfortunately, we don't have a picture of Thomas, Rufus's first child with Roxana. However, we do have a picture of Warren, Roxana, and Rufus. Rufus was part of the Southern gentry, which means he was at the highest caliber of Southern society—a brigadier general. But this also means that he, nor anyone else, couldn't escape human desires, emotions, lust, feelings, etc. Another similarly situated brigadier general was John Robert Jones of Harrisonburg, Virginia. In her book *Freedom's Child*, Ms. Carrie Allen McCray indicates that she found out that her grandfather was General Jones, a brigadier general: "'Grandfather,' I exclaimed, not quite ready to accept that truth. I learned later that Rosemary had had difficulty with that too. In telling the story of our trip when were back home, she said, 'Carrie found out who her grandfather was.' I laughed and reminded her that he was her grandfather too."[39] The record also indicates that Jones was also involved in the Battle of Chancellorsville. Whether he was there at the same time as Barringer or not is a matter for further review. We must remember that Barringer was wounded several times. In the case of Jones, we also see that he had two black families. How is it possible for white men to fight and die to uphold slavery but at the same time have black children? This may make sense if one remembers that slaves were not considered people, only property. How will we, as a country, overcome this way of thinking? Our young people, as I can see as a college instructor, will be having a rough time reconciling this part of our history once they learn the true facts of our history.

Thank God we, as a country, are trying to reconcile our perceived or actual differences; but it is very clear that we cannot escape our history or humanity without looking back. As some of our brothers on the street would say, "It is what it is." And we will have to face it head-on in the near future.

Coleman's Legal Legacy

As one begins to understand the environment that Coleman lived in, it is important to acknowledge that Coleman's father was a full-blown attorney, and some of his skills must have affected Coleman. In fact, Sheridan makes this point: "On June 13, 1843, Barringer obtained his license to practice law. To become licensed, he had [*sic*] taken a nine-hour written and oral examination administered by Supreme Court judges in Raleigh, NC."[40] Buying and selling real estate was clearly one of those skills. Coleman must have also learned about the legal profession from his master, William Coleman. It should be noted that William's father, Daniel Coleman, was also an attorney; and he worked for the Treasury Department in 1876, one hundred years after the American Revolution. Moreover, Sheridan states that before the Civil War, both Rufus Barringer and Daniel Coleman were the mayors of Concord. The family, including Roxana, must have laid the foundation for Concord in a very unique manner. She further discussed, "Rufus, who shunned running for state or national office, was elected mayor of Concord on January 31, 1857, 1858 and also 1859. Later Daniel Coleman was also elected as mayor." In 1857, Coleman was eight years old; and his brother, Thomas, was twelve years old. Before going over the activities of General Barringer after the war, a major point was raised by his relative S. R. Barringer. He states, "Although there is no direct documentation that proves Rufus was the father of the two boys, it was a matter of general knowledge in the Concord area."[41] What documentation would one need? A birth certificate for a sexual relationship with a chattel slave was not possible. If they were not the children of General Barringer, why discuss Warren's various attributes? "While Rufus became active in state politics again, his mulatto son Warren Clay Coleman, (probably under William Coleman's and/or Rufus Barringer's guidance,) bought land in the black areas of Concord and erected rental houses."[42]

I surmise that a conversation with Warren and Rufus would have taken place as follows:

> COLEMAN. I am thinking about buying some real estate, do you agree?
>
> RUFUS. Yes, I think that it would be a good idea, and I will give you a loan. But you should not tell anyone.

One point not mentioned in other books about Coleman is the fact that he was surrounded by legal professionals. Number 1 was his father, Rufus Barringer. He was an attorney who also served in the state legislature, starting in 1848, a year before Warren was born. On the

Coleman side of the family, there is Daniel Coleman (an attorney) and his son and Coleman's master, William Coleman. On the Barringer side of the family, Rufus's two brothers, Paul and Victor, were also attorneys. (See the Coleman/Barringer historical family tree juxtaposed with black history in 1895 on page). It is no wonder that Warren felt comfortable with legal activities involving real estate and others. This is especially true when Coleman remained on the Coleman farm until 1870 or four to five years after the end of the Civil War. Coleman was twenty-one years old in 1870. In the Krieger book, we also see that once he returned to the country, his master agreed to tutor Coleman; and the master also encouraged him to go to Howard University. After returning from the Civil War, we see that General Rufus Barringer sold real estate, and he was involved in various forms of real estate management in Charlotte, North Carolina. The Barringer name is seen in many of parts of Charlotte. Specifically, in an article in the *Charlotte Democrat* published on August 17, 1874, we see that General Barringer was engaged in the selling of a major piece of real estate: "I offer at private sale a body of valuable land lying on McAlpine's Creek adjoining R.B. Wallace, being part of the old J.J. Maxwell farm. The track contains over 300 acres."[43] As some would say, "The fruit does not fall too far from the tree."

How many former black slaves could say that their father (whom they knew) was a practicing attorney? In the same newspaper, we see that Rufus, through his connection with the Morrision family, sold property on Davidson College (it was known as Andrews House and Lot) and provided farms for rent. And during his death, he was identified as such: "He was a great student and careful reader who did not hide his light under a bushel." How this quote relates to my quote in chapter 1 has blown my mind. Barringer's legacy is an amazing part of Coleman's life that most people are unaware of, but it does explain why Coleman behaved in a manner that would impress most attorneys and demonstrated that this legacy (hidden from most) is why he became a very rich man. Moreover, in the Feldman book, we see that his master, William Coleman, was involved in training Coleman: "When he got back to Concord in 1865, Coleman began to be tutored by his old master, who by then had come back from Germany."[23] Feldman also makes the point that Coleman's master also encouraged Coleman to attend Howard University.

White Resistance to Black Advancement

It must also be revealed that Paul did not think too much of black people. In short, he made statements indicating that education for blacks was a waste. Why would he say that? He must have known that his father bore two children with an African-American slave. In line with this fact, according to Norrell, Paul stated, "Barringer declared, and thus black education promoted racial warfare."[44] Paul Barringer, like many others, felt that educating blacks and otherwise trying to help them was fruitless. Another man, John Temple Graves, advocated that all blacks should be rounded up and deposited into the far West. Another man, Ben Tillman, made various statements indicating that under the skin, blacks were savages. These sentiments were feelings that Washington, Coleman, and Douglass were facing on a daily basis. Men like James K. Vardaman, J. Thomas Heflin, and Ollie James of Kentucky were constantly opposing the attempts of Washington and others to uplift blacks in the South; and they also took their message oftentimes to the North. Given that blacks were fighting among themselves, it must be noted that the resistance from whites was even more severe. Unfortunately, many blacks like myself would say that not much has changed.

Lynching

One of the most severe actions to prevent black advancement was lynching. Of course, this was a horrendous way to die, and anyone can understand that lynching was very debilitating. Because lynching was so bad, people like Washington, an associate of Coleman, attempted to do everything possible to have whites denounce this type of behavior. Specifically, in Alabama, W. D. Jelks denounced the practice in 1903, the same year the Coleman Mill was in full operation. However, years later, Governor Jelks changed his tune and made several negative comments about education for blacks, including the efforts of Tuskegee.[45] Washington was disappointed.

Violence after Reconstruction was bloody. We also see that the Colfax Massacre cost the lives of 105 people in 1874. Moreover, we also see both the Hamburg Massacre and the Ellenton Riot wherein over eighty black men lost their lives in total.[46] The record makes it clear that lynching was a normal occurrence in America, especially in the South. Specifically from 1889 to 1932, 3,745 people were lynched. Given this information as we look at the life of Coleman from 1889 to 1904, he must had understood that black men were being influenced by the behavior of white men. The record also indicates that if a black man was successful in business and others, he could be a target of very harsh treatment like lynching. Most of the time, black men were lynched, but there have been occasions when whites were also lynched. "Sometimes white people were lynched. In 1891 in New Orleans, 11 Italian were lynched for alleged involvement with the Mafia and for the murder of the city's police chief."[47] Some people would say that for some people, Italians are similar to blacks. In the late 1880s and the early 1900s, violence or lynching was widespread. In 1886, there was a conflict between blacks and whites in Washington County, Texas, and three black men were lynched. In the town of Phoenix, South Carolina, in 1898, there was another conflict; and an unknown number of black men were killed. Most famously, there is the case in Wilmington where "a white mob destroyed the newspaper office. Black and white officials resigned in a vain attempt to prevent further violence, but at least a dozen black men—and perhaps more—were murdered. Some 1,500 black residents of Wilmington fled."[48] And yet in another part of the South (New Orleans), another case of brutality took place. In 1900, at the same time that the Coleman Mill was about to develop a product, a man by the name of Robert Charles was beaten by a police officer. In the end, twenty-seven white people were killed, Charles was killed, and about a dozen blacks were killed and others injured.

Ku Klux Klan

The work of the Ku Klux Klan is another matter in the realm of violence against African-Americans. For this group of people, having blacks stay in the homes and do nothing but work in the fields or do whatever whites wanted was the ideal situation. The Klan was founded one year after the Civil War (1866). The Klan represented whites from all walks of life, and some branches were near Coleman's home of Mecklenburg County, North Carolina. Coleman must have known about this group and its intent to limit the accomplishments of black people. People like Benjamin F. Randolph, Lee Nance, and Solomon G. W. Dill were killed to send a message to the black community.29 York County, South Carolina, according to record, was a place where nearly all the white men belonged to the Klan. Years later, blacks were subjected to a new insult in the form of a movie: *The Birth of a Nation*. As a work of cinema, the film was considered a masterpiece. Even President Wilson agreed to have it played in the White House. W. E. B Du Bois complained in the *Crisis* that in the film, "The Negro was represented either as an ignorant fool, a vicious rapist, a venal or unscrupulous politician or a faithful but doddering idiot."49 After the airing of *The Birth of Nation*, the Klan, which was diminished, was able to revive itself at Stone Mountain, Georgia. Thank God a person like Ida B. Wells was around to speak out against this horrid illegal behavior.

As we look at the time when Coleman was trying to develop the mill, it is very clear that violence must have been at the top of his mind. Because Coleman did not write his autobiography like Douglass and Washington, we will never know his true feelings about a host of topics. First and foremost, Coleman was a businessman, not an abolitionist and not an educator; and on top of everything, he was biracial. However, Washington and Douglass were also fathered by white men whom they did not know. We also know that Coleman was trained by his master and his father. Both may have also given him money to buy real estate in Concord, North Carolina, which we will discuss later in the book. We also know that when Coleman was getting a brief education at Howard, he met important people like John Dancy, T. Thomas Fortune, and many others. Clearly, the main point is that Warren C. Coleman was living in a world where blacks were not expected to be successful in any form or any way.

Ida B. Wells-Barnett

Wells was born into slavery in 1862. What did Frederick Douglass, Booker T. Washington, Warren C. Coleman, and Ida B. Wells have in common? They were all born into slavery. One was an abolitionist and orator, one was an educator, one was a black entrepreneur, and Mrs. Barnett was an anti-lynching crusader. Ms. Wells's primary issue was lynching and the horror that came with this type of behavior. In 1892, two black men were defending their store in Memphis, Tennessee. They killed several white men. The black men were arrested and were later lynched by a white mob, just like we see in Concord in 1898. Given the Memphis incident, Wells wrote an in-depth report about lynching in the newspaper operated by T. Thomas Fortune.

Frederick Douglass was also one of her supporters. Wells attended school at Shaw and Fisk University. In 1898, the same time when Coleman was building his mill, Wells confronted President William McKinley and demanded that he make the necessary reforms to stop lynching in the South and other parts of the country. Wells later married Ferdinand Barnett, and she was thereafter known as Ida B. Wells-Barnett. They had four children. Wells was married and confronting the leadership of the country during the same time frame when a lynching was taking place in Concord, North Carolina. Like Joseph C. Price, Bishop J. W. Hood, and others, Wells went to Britain seeking support for her anti-lynching crusade. Given this history of going outside the country for assistance, why would anyone think that America will endure reparations for African-Americans now or anytime in the near future? Affirmative action, one could say is a small way to compensate for the damages, has also become a bad or negative concept.

Mr. Bakke made it clear that he did not think blacks should be favored over him when it came to admission into college. During his time, he wanted everyone to be treated the same even though there was no level playing field for blacks, Native Americans, and others mistreated by the government. Another source provides additional information about the work of Mrs. Wells-Barnett. As a journalist and newspaper publisher, Wells traveled throughout the South documenting and writing about the unjust lynching of black men. She chronicled each case—keeping records, pulling police files, and interviewing witnesses (*Chicago Tribune*, June 14, 2019, by Lolly Bowean). Wells was also a champion of the suffrage movement. Due to her efforts to save black men and women from the horrors of lynching, how many books and articles were written by her and by others?[50] The number is quite numerous, and Wells is truly a leader of the early African-American community that was trying to fight racism and remain viable in a hostile country that made it clear that black people were not equal to whites. Wells died at the age of sixty-nine in 1931. The record also indicates that Wells was also being considered for the leadership of black America, but her gender was a major obstacle. During the time when Coleman's mill was under development, Wells had four children. Fortunately, her legacy is well, and black Americans owe her a debt of gratitude for taking on a topic that many did not want to discuss. "While remaining active in many endeavors Wells-Barnett and her husband had four children, Charles in 1896, Herman in 1897, Ida in 1901 and Alfreda in 1904."[51]

Chapter Four

Coleman's Life as an Entrepreneur and Philanthropist for Colleges and Churches

Know, do and be happy
—Bishop J. W. Hood

A Real Estate Mogul

After starting his career as a small businessman, Coleman is most famous for owning various lots of real estate, as noted previously in an exchange with Mr. Odell and many others. In addition to his activities in the store, his main business occupation was buying, investing, owning, renting, and selling real estate. As an affluent real estate owner, Coleman owned four farms and close to one hundred houses in what is now known as the bottom, along Lincoln Street and other parts of Concord. Because of his lucrative lifestyle, Coleman was able to build a home on Church and Cabarrus Avenue, which was not far from one of the Barringers' home on Union (where the Cannon Library stands and there is a state marker). I am certain he (Coleman) knew that Victor Barringer was his half-brother, living nearby. Coleman's home was on Church and Cabarrus (formerly Depot), and a picture of it can be seen at the Concord Carolina Mall (see page).

Why were the Barringers' and Colemans' houses torn down while the houses of Cannon and Odell were preserved? How can we remedy this obvious injustice or oversight? The record shows that Coleman's lots/houses were located as follows: According to the "Estate Record of Warren C. Coleman" by Sallie R. Johnson (collected in 1904),[52] Coleman had lots in Cabarrus County on the east and south side of Depot Street (currently known as Cabarrus Avenue). A lot was also located on the north side of Depot nearby Scotia Seminary. Moreover, Coleman owned lots on Spring Street, West Corbin, Prospect, Lincoln, McGill (formerly known as Beatties Ford Road), and many others located in an area known as Coleburg. In addition, there were lots 3, 4, 7, 8, 13, 14, 15, 16, etc., on Tournment Street. In addition to numerous lots in Cabarrus County, Coleman also owned lots outside Cabarrus County, including lots in Monroe, Forsyth, Greensboro, and Rowan County. One lot would be one or more acres. In summary, when one looks at the property owned by Coleman, to say that he was a small property owner would clearly be an understatement.

In 1883, at the North Carolina Industrial Association in Raleigh, as noted State in the Chronicle of November 17, 1883, we see that Coleman was a rich man admired by many: "Warren C. Coleman of Concord had on exhibition where four beautiful cream colored horses were admired by everybody."[53] In comparison, if a black man showed up today with four cars worth $40,000 or more in Concord, most people would admire him and stand in awe. Moreover, at various fairs in New Bern, North Carolina, Coleman exhibited "a four-year cow that gave four gallons of milk a watermelon that weighted fifty-seven pounds and a cantalope that weighed thirty-five pounds.[54]

Rev. Frank Logan

By the late 1890s, another great man was working to develop a viable public school system in Concord. His name was Rev. Frank Logan. He was born in Greensboro, North Carolina. Logan was born on November 19, 1859, which means he was ten years younger than Coleman. Logan served the Concord school system for forty years from

1891 until 1932. Rev. Logan clearly knew Coleman, and I am certain that they collaborated to further the education of African-American children during the late nineteenth century and twentieth century. The current mill owner, Bill Bryant, indicated that he remembers seeing information in the mill indicating that young girls were also involved in the mill, for training and others. Where did that history (the story of girls and children working in the mill) go?

Rev. Logan helped to establish the Logan School, and he was the first principal in 1891. This was the same year that Coleman was working in Concord to establish his real estate empire, working in his store and doing whatever he could to assist schools and colleges in the Concord community. Rev. Logan was married three times. Logan was also the pastor of the historic Bellefonte Presbyterian Church. He also served as the chaplain of Scotia College. By 1924, the Logan School moved from the original wooden structure into a modern brick building with ten classrooms and a spacious auditorium that held four hundred students. Within five years, the high school was accredited, and Rev. Logan retired in 1932. In 1960, the Logan School became a full member of the Southern Association of Colleges and Schools. Other principals included E. L. James, C. C. Griffin, and last but not the least, Allen T. Small. Logan and his wife are buried in the OCGC with over two hundred other people. The Logan School closed in 1970 due to the Supreme Court's decision on *Brown v. Board of Education.* Included as a black school was the Shankletown School, which was established in 1913. The first principal was Fred Duncan, and the school was closed in the 1960s.[55]

Higher Education in Concord

The Zion Wesley Institute's (now Livingstone College) first session in one room next to Scotia College in Concord, North Carolina, was established after Joseph C. Price returned from Europe with a contribution of over $10,000. Rev. Price was the first president of the college. Livingstone College was established in Concord, North Carolina, by the AME Zion Church but later moved to Salisbury, North Carolina. Therefore, the record indicates that there were three colleges, one was also sponsored by the Lutheran community, for African-Americans in Concord in the late 1800s. Another was Livingstone, and the third was Scotia.

Given Mr. Coleman's wealth, he was able to give financial assistance to schools like Howard University, Livingstone College, Shaw University, Scotia College (founded by Rev. Luke Dorland, who was a Presbyterian pastor), and many others. There was also a Coleman school in Wellford, South Carolina. There were about two thousand people living in Wellford in 2010. Burgess also makes the point that Coleman assisted Zion Wesley College (now Livingstone College) with a loan in 1880, and it was paid back by 1886 with great flexibility on the terms to assist the college. As such, while the Morrisons were developing Davidson College, Coleman was helping to develop Livingstone College. The connection could not be more vivid. Coleman's half sister Eugenia is one connection, and Warren is the other. Both are tied together by their father, Rufus.

Working with the AME Zion Church

The record is clear that Coleman made a major difference for the City of Concord and especially the AME Zion Church. Today, three of his many great legacies remain. The Zion Hill AME Zion Church is one, and Price Memorial AME Zion Church on Spring Street is another. The Old Camp Ground Cemetery (OCGC), which stands on Cabarrus near the Martin Luther King Memorial roundabout, is a third. The MLK monument is mentioned on traffic signs, but there's no mention of the OCGC. Why? Could it be that in a few years, OCGC will no longer exist? What is wrong with the leaders of Concord? What is wrong with the people of the many churches supported by people on that site? Why are we so willing to just forget? Someone or somebody must take responsibility. I tried to do my part, and it was not welcomed. Others have also tried to offer help, and it has not been accepted. Why? Prior to becoming the main supporter of Price Memorial, Coleman provided enormous support for Zion Hill AME. Zion Hill was located near Dorland Street, right off Cabarrus Avenue. Zion Hill was later relocated to Skipwith Street due to a major storm (Hugo). According to historical records, Zion Hill AME Zion Church owns OCGC. What is going on for the sake of the people of Concord, the people of North Carolina, and the people of America?

Bishop James Walker Hood

One of the key people when one looks at the early churches in North Carolina is Bishop J. W. Hood. Hood was born in Chester Counter, Pennsylvania, on May 30, 1831. Bishop Hood and Coleman may have had a conversation that went like this:

> HOOD. You need to get some higher education. Without it, you will not be respected.

> COLEMAN. You are right. Will you give me a letter of reference?"

> HOOD. No problem, as a member of the Zion community, you will be accepted without a problem.

Previously, I mentioned that when Coleman went to Howard University, in his possession was a letter of reference from Rev. J. W. Hood. As a lifelong friend and associate, records also show that Rev. Hood was on the incorporation papers for the mill in 1896/1897. Both of these events demonstrate that Bishop Hood was a positive lifelong mentor for Coleman. Given his assistance with the mill, Hood and Coleman may have had the following discussion:

> COLEMAN. I need your assistance in the incorporation of the mill. Will you assist me?

> HOOD. Given my assistance in helping you to attend Howard University, I am very impressed that you want to take this next step in life, and your willingness to help our people is outstanding.

COLEMAN. I know that it will be difficult, but our people are unable to work in the white mills, and I have the connections and means to make a difference.

Bishop Hood was also a mentor for Dr. Price, and this can be said when we see Bishop Hood and Dr. Price working together in England to acquire the money to establish Livingstone College in 1882. Their conversation may have been as follows:

HOOD. You are a great educator and orator, and I know you can get the resources we need.

PRICE. I will do everything in my power because our people will not be able to progress without education.

According to Burgess, we also see that in 1865, right after the war, the leader of a black convention in Raleigh was James Walker Hood.3
Not a long time ago in 2019, during a lunch with a prominent white Methodist pastor, he wondered why there were not many or any predominately black United Methodist Churches in Cabarrus County. I replied, "The absence is due to Bishop J. W. Hood, who was responsible for spreading the word of the AME Zion Church in many places in the North and South and especially North Carolina." Rev. Hood was born in Chester County, Pennsylvania, on May 30, 1831, setting the foundation for many of the institutions that we see today in many parts of North Carolina in the field of religion, education, etc. The Hood Theological Seminary in Salisbury remains as a continuous prime example of his legacy, given the thousands of people who have been educated under his name. Hood made a major difference in the development of Livingstone College and presided over the board of trustees, and six of his children were enrolled in the college. Moreover, Robinson makes this point: "He [Hood] was sent to North Carolina in 1863, and during his ministry, over five hundred churches were erected under his supervision. Hood was one of the most effective black missionaries and organizers in North Carolina."4 Before the Brown decision on school integration, Hood indicated that black children may not do well due to the behavior of white administrators. The evidence

in this book supports the concern expressed by Hood in the nineteenth century. Hood also spent a lot of his time in Virginia, South Carolina, and Georgia. During his early career, Hood also spent time in Nova Scotia, Canada.

As we look at the life of J. W. Hood, Frederick Douglass, Booker T. Washington, Dr. Joseph C. Price, and Warren C. Coleman, it is clear that these men were working against the odds. What if they were allowed to freely move around like white people during their time? What if they were not segregated into little corners of the society? A man like Barack Obama demonstrated what black leadership could do. Relative to our current president (Trump), the difference is striking and speaks to the fact that America has turned to a racist point of view. This difference is a clear example of white privilege. This difference in leadership and/or opportunity is what black people have had to deal with during their entire existence in North America. What man would want to compete with Barack Obama? Presidents like Lincoln, FDR, or Kennedy may be at the same level. It is going to be interesting to see how Obama is treated historically over the next twenty to thirty years. Please let me know (smile).

Membership at Zion Chapel

According to J. K. Rouse, the record indicates that Warren C. Coleman, Richard McCree, John Young, and Ephraim Means were trustees at Zion Hill and involved in the purchase of the OCGC.[56]

Zion Hill AME Zion Church, first known as Zion Chapel, is known as the oldest black church in Cabarrus County. It was founded in 1859, two years before the start of the Civil War. Coleman and his wife were part of the original membership. This church, coupled with the leadership of Dr. Joseph C. Price, was able to develop Livingstone College, which currently operates in Salisbury, North Carolina, but was first established in Concord when Price returned from England. According to Mr. Robinson, the first location was located accordingly: "The property was located on the south side of Depot Street, adjoining the land of Dr. Luke Dorland and C.N. Wager."[57] Additional pastors of Zion Hill included P. B. McCain, Smith Clairborn, A. J. Rogers, ggs, and Rev. J. E. O Eason. Clearly, when one talks about the town of Concord, the Zion Hill AME Zion Church must be included with admiration and pride. After deciding to leave Zion Hill and open a new church on Spring Street in 1895, the same year of the great Atlanta Exposition, Mr. Coleman must have thought about who or what he would want to name the church after. I am certain that many people must have come to his mind. Maybe some of the people connected to the mill or others unknown to history but close to him. After some thought, Mr. Coleman decided on Dr. Joseph C. Price. Why?

Dr. Joseph C. Price

Dr. Price was born in 1854, which means that Dr. Price was five years younger than Mr. Coleman and twenty-three years younger than J. W. Hood. Dr. Price would have been five years older than Rev. Frank Logan (another great leader in Concord). Dr. Price died in 1893 or two years prior to the great exposition in 1895. His death changed history. Price was only thirty-nine years old when he passed, which explains why he did not write an autobiography similar to Washington and Douglass (see copy of "Education and the Problem" that he made in July 10, 1890, or three years before his unfortunate death).

Dr. Price was born in Elizabeth City, North Carolina, but his mark was made in Concord and Salisbury where he was selected as the first president of Livingstone College. It must be understood that Livingstone College, as stated previously, started operating in Concord, near Scotia College. In 1890, Dr. Price later became the president of the new national organization called the National Afro-American League. It was founded by New York City editor Thomas Fortune. Thomas Fortune was the same person who went to Howard University with Mr. Coleman. It is clear that all these men knew one another and became aware of their work accordingly. The league was a precursor to the NAACP formed in the early 1900s.

Price had two grandsons. One was Charles P. Sherrill, and the other was Dr. Richard W. Sherrill. Price was, in accordance with a poll by eight thousand subscribers of the *Indianapolis Freeman*, selected as one of the ten greatest Negroes who ever lived. The record also indicates that Price, unlike Booker T. Washington, did not want to compromise the rights of blacks to get along and live with whites. In one of Price's famous speeches in an event held in Minneapolis in July 1890 (three years before his death) to the National Education Association (NEA), he makes several points. He indicates that blacks have made tremendous progress since the end of the Civil War. Price also makes the point advocated by many black intellectuals today that whites must also be educated about race and its implications. In his speech about the problem, Price states that the South will suffer if Negroes are not educated appropriately. He continues to make the point that slavery, about 250 years, has made a deep impression; and there is a lot of work to be done to remedy the problem, which remains today in 2019. Dr. Price's home remains at 828 West Monroe in Salisbury, North Carolina. Because he was the first president of Livingstone College, it was important for the college to preserve it accordingly.

The record indicates that because of Dr. Price's educational accomplishments and great oratory, he was able to receive the amount requested ($10,000) under the leadership of Bishop Hood. Hood had to leave England early and left Dr. Price with the task of acquiring the money needed to start the school. In gratitude, Dr. Price agreed to name the school after a great son of England, Dr. Stanley Livingstone. According to Lenwood Davis, "When Price was in England, the London Times called him the 'The World Orator.' He stayed in England for a year and when he returned home in 1882, he had raised $10,000.00 above the expenses for Zion Wesley Institute (now Livingstone College)."[58]

Price having a legacy in Concord and Salisbury and various other places only makes sense due to his activities and history in the area. Price was an awesome person in the African-American community, and his legacy is real and remains in Concord and Salisbury for the world to see. However, because he died at an early age, he was not able to fulfill his maximum potential as a black professional. If he had not died in 1893, we might be talking about the Livingstone Red Tails and the Livingstone Air Men. Given the evidence currently on hand, my position is that Coleman knew that Dr. Price was in line to become the new leader of black America. However, Coleman was also a friend of

Booker T. Washington; and because Dr. Price died two years earlier, he could still honor Dr. Price by naming Price Temple Church after Dr. Price, which still remains in Concord North Carolina, at 192 Spring Street SW.

Price Temple

The Price Temple was later renamed Price Memorial AME Zion Church and remains open up to this day. I am honored to be one of the trustees as of 2016. According to Price Memorial's short history of the Price, "Price Memorial is one of the remaining churches on the Concord District that has retained its original architectural structure. The exterior of the church was completed with a stucco finish and painted light gray. Through the years, various additions and repairs have been made. In 1946, the interior of the church was enlarged and refurbished. In 1954, an education building was constructed consisting of a furnace room, a first floor with six classrooms, ladies lounge, bell tower/usher's room, two restrooms, and a second floor housing the fellowship hall, a kitchen, a library and a church office, in addition see Price Memorial A.M.E Zion church on page." In addition, Norrell also makes it clear that Dr. Price was in line to become the new leader: "A more likely successor to Douglass might have been Joseph Charles Price, a preacher and the founder of Livingstone College in Salisbury, North Carolina."[59] If Price had lived, how would history have been changed? My mind continues to wonder. On a letter developed by several church members, it is noted that Price Temple grew from a small one-room cottage, built by its gifted members, to the present-day structure.

Under the leadership of Rev. J. H. C. Blue, Dr. George I. Blackwell, Rev. I. B. Turner, Dr. Jewell I. Walker, Rev. Reynard Ruston, Rev. A. A. Speight, Rev. J. Ruth Davis, and many others too numerous to mention, to its current structure. Clearly, this church and its legacy can proudly take its place in American history. I feel very proud knowing that I have made a small contribution to the City of Concord and the AME Zion Church in North Carolina. (Also see the Price Memorial historical tree on page.)

Thomas Fortune

"Thomas Fortune was a good friend of Booker T. Washington."12 According to Gates, Fortune's "mother died in 1868, and his father, who worked as a carpenter made investments in real estate that allowed him to provide for his children while remaining active in politics until his death in 1897." Moreover, the same source reveals that Fortune and Washington recognized Fortune's exceptional talent and hired him to ghostwrite *A New Negro for a New Century* and *The Negro in Business*. As such, there was no surprise that Fortune, with the death of Price, recommended that he (Washington) become the leader of the race. Fortune became the ultimate kingmaker in 1895. Fortune became the leader of the Afro-American Council. As such, Fortune came under severe criticism from people like William Monroe Trotter and others who felt that Fortune was in the Washington camp.

During the early 1900s, Fortune was known as a heavy drinker. Due to his overall behavior, Washington became unhappy with Fortune and decided to try to influence how Fortune's paper was written and what was being said. In 1906, in line with the violence erupting in Atlanta, Georgia, Fortune advocated violence in a similar way to what Malcolm X spoke of in the 1960s. Fortune spoke of an eye for an eye. The late 1890s and early 1900s were times of violence in various parts of the country, as noted in chapter 3. Down the road, Fortune found himself working for my hometown newspaper, the *Amsterdam News*. Fortune, in this regard, remained in the Washington camp and began to become critical of Du Bois and other developers of the NAACP for allowing whites to become leaders of the race. In the long run, the NAACP became the primary advocate for African-American rights in the courts, at the movies, and various other locations. It is also noted that Fortune was very helpful to Washington in developing the National Negro Business League. At the first meeting, thirty states were represented, and the size demonstrated that a national organization was at hand. However, Washington and Fortune later split with regard to support for Teddy Roosevelt. Fortune advocated strongly for an independent party, whereas people like Du Bois advocated (while holding his nose) for the election of William Jennings Bryan. As Fortune traveled through his life, he often would express anger and frustration about white mobs and how they were treating African-Americans, especially in the South. Specifically, Fortune remained a friend of Washington; however, in several sources, we find this: "But Fortune's friendship came at a cost. He was reportedly drunk when he declared that blacks in Wilmington should kill whites in retribution."[60] Because of these sentiments and his overall posture as a drunk, it is no wonder that Fortune was unsung, and his career as a kingmaker had been lost, but not forgotten. As Washington and Fortune expressed different views in the aftermath of Wilmington, Coleman was in the process of building his mill. In this regard, one must ask, Why did Coleman continue to feel that his mill could make a difference in light of the violence engulfing the black community? I believe he did so because he knew about the work of Douglass, Washington, Du Bois, and many others and felt that building the mill, in spite of the odds, would advance the cause of blacks trying to prevail and establish themselves as men in America.

W. E. B. Du Bois

When one looks at the Washington Papers, it is clear that Du Bois had a relationship with Washington. The relationship depended upon the issues at hand. For the most part, Du Bois was known as Washington's primary critic, and history has highlighted their differences. Du Bois was the major critic, but others like William Hannibal Thomas also raised objections to Washington and his compromise posture. History indicates that Du Bois and Washington were often at odds because Washington was seen by many as the leader of black America. They said, "That was the real issue: Washington's standing as the leader of the race. Du Bois, Villard, Spingarn and other insiders at the NAACP continued to view Washington as an opponent because most Americans, including most blacks, still considered him the preeminent black man among them."[61]

Although it is understood that Washington and Du Bois were often at odds, by 1900, Du Bois visited Tuskegee. This is the same time when Coleman was about to start producing goods in his mill in Concord. How Coleman would have negotiated a meeting with Washington and Du Bois at the time would be interesting. This is especially true when one looks at Du Bois's educational background. Du Bois went to Fisk for undergraduate school but then returned to Massachusetts to get a second baccalaureate degree from Harvard. He studied at the University of Berlin before becoming the first African-American to receive a doctorate of philosophy from Harvard. The difference between the Southern blacks and the Northern blacks could not be more stark. This difference unfortunately remains among some people until this day. My question to anyone reading this book is whether conflicts between Northern blacks and Southern blacks are something we can't afford. The problems for blacks are so great, in my mind, that working together is critical. When an African-American is shot in the street or otherwise killed, the killer does not care what part of the country the person is from. The person is black (assuming the other person is white) and assumed to be a criminal—that is it. This was true during the time of slavery and Jim Crow, and it is true today. "By 1900 the most distinguished black scholar in the United States, Du Bois was vastly better educated than Washington (and Coleman) Du Bois admired European culture, whereas Washington assumed that American way of life was inherently better. Du Bois appreciated cities and universities as the places that fostered thought and culture. Washington was suspicious of urban life and assumed that the best places in America, especially for blacks, were rural."[62] I could understand why most Northern black Americans would have a problem with this feeling; however, when one looks at his (Washington's) place of business, it only makes sense that he would feel that way. It only makes sense to me that Coleman, living and working on the outskirts of Charlotte in Concord, North Carolina, with the hostility of whites in his face, would feel the same way. However, I tend to ignore this conflict with Northern blacks and Southern blacks, which I have felt myself, for the greater good of trying to assist the larger black community.

As Price Memorial continues to survive as a small church regardless of the difficult external economic conditions, clearly the spirit of Warren C. Coleman remains in the building—and in me and others. This statement is important because many churches within the Concord District are struggling financially, and attracting younger members is important for all the churches to continue to survive in one form or another. I pray that the black community will not forget the many churches that served their community when blacks were not welcome in an equal manner in white churches. Moving forward, the role of the black church remains important and must be overwhelmingly supported by the entire community.

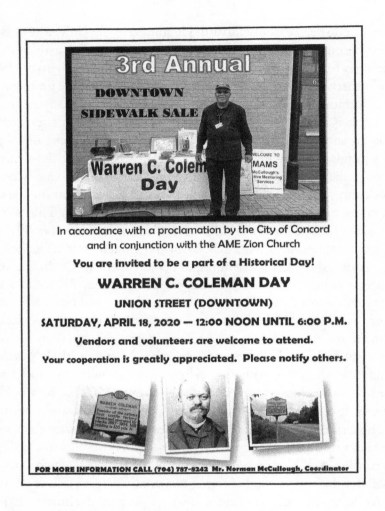

Celebrating Warren C. Coleman

Saturday, February 23 (1:00 p.m.)

Local educator and mentor Norman J. McCullough shares insights on Warren C. Coleman's place in history and his relevance to young people today.

Come find out why McCullough thinks Concord's pioneering African-American textile mill owner deserves to be known across the nation.

(1890) Joseph C. Price, "Education and the Problem"

Joseph C. Price emerged in the 1880s as one of the most celebrated educators and orators in black America. Born free in North Carolina in 1854, Price attended Lincoln University in Pennsylvania where he garnered numerous oratorical prizes and graduated as valedictorian in 1879. Two years later, as a delegate of the AME Zion Church to the World's Ecumenical Conference of Methodism held in London, he delivered an unscheduled speech from the floor that created a sensation. And soon afterward, he was called the World's Orator by the British press. One of Price's most important orations was given at the annual meeting of the National Education Association (NEA) held in Minneapolis on July 10–12, 1890. That speech appears below:

> If I had a thousand tongues and each tongue were a thousand thunderbolts and each thunderbolt had a thousand voices, I would use them all to help you understand a loyal and misrepresented and misjudged people. The real question implied in this subject, as I understand it, is, Will education solve the race problem? With such an idea in view it is but

proper we have some conception of what the problem is, in order that we may select the best means for its solution; for it is evident that all remedies, whether for the removal of disorders in the body, or in the social state—whether in physianthropy or sociology—must be in proportion to their affected parts or abnormal conditions. It is further observable that the length of time a malady is allowed to grow, or an evil condition is permitted to exist and develop baneful results, has much to do with the nature of the forces that will neutralize the growth or destroy the evil. It is not infrequently the case that the age of a complaint or an undesirable state of affairs has to determine, to a very large degree, the means of resistance, or the remedies which will effect the cure. More is true. As it is admitted that time is a large element in the stubbornness of a condition or evil, so it is also true that time, coupled with the highest wisdom of administration, becomes an indispensable element in producing the healthier and more desirable conditions. It is further patent to every thoughtful mind that there are complex irregularities in the human system, as in the body politic, that no single remedy or manner of procedure can regulate. In such cases we have to proceed step by step, and take only one phase of the complaint at a time; and the remedies that are efficient in one stage are totally inadequate to the other. Each stage has its peculiar prescription—some requiring milder, and others severer antidotes; and whenever these antidotes are used substitutionally, we are thwarted in our desired end, and our purposes often miscarry. The negro problem is different from the Indian or Chinese question. In the negro, we find a commendable absence of all the stubborn and discordant characteristics which are peculiar to the Indian or the Chinaman; and the negro suffrage demands universal education. It cannot be said, as it was stated fifty years ago, that a negro cannot be educated. The history of education among the colored people for a quarter of a century does not confirm the statement. The noble men and women who went into the South as missionaries, and felt their way through the smoke of battle and stepped over crimson battle fields and among the wounded and the dying to bring intelligence to the negroes, were taunted as going on a fool's errand. But the tens of thousands of young men and women in the schools of high grade established by Northern service and philanthropy—a million negro children in the public schools of the South—are an imperishable monument to the wisdom of their action. I again quote from Dr. Haygood, who is an authority on this subject: "All told, fully fifty millions of dollars have gone into the work of their (negro) education since 1865. Of this fifty millions, more than half has been Southern money." The negroes have made more progress in elementary and other education during these twenty three years than any other illiterate people in the world, and they have justified the philanthropy and public policy that made the expenditure.

WHITES MUST BE EDUCATED, AS WELL.

It must be remembered, however, that there is more to be done than education of the blacks, as a solution to the race problem; for much of the stubbornness of the question is involved in the ignorant, lawless and vicious whites of the South, who need education worse than many of the blacks. To educate one race and neglect the other, is to leave the problem half solved, for there is a class of whites in the South, to some extent, more and hopeless in their mental and moral condition than the negro. This is the to which many of the actual outrages are more attributable than to any other class. Educate these, as well as the blacks, and our problem is shorn of its strength. When we call to mind the fact that seventy per cent of the colored vote in the South is illiterate, and thirty per cent of the white vote in the same condition, it is not difficult for one to discern that education of blacks and whites, as well, is not only necessary for the solution of the race problem and for good government, but for the progress and prosperity of that section where such illiteracy obtains.

For the safety of the republic, the perpetuity of its glory and the stability of its institutions are commensurate, with the intelligence and morality of its citizens, whether they be black men or white men.

THE POVERTY OF THE NEGRO

The poverty of the negro is another stubborn element of the problem. It is urged that the wealth and intelligence of the South must not suffer a man, if he is poor and black, to exercise the prerogatives of American citizenship. Strange doctrine this, in a republic which is a refuge for the oppressed from lands under the sun, and the so called land of the free! But will education help to remove this objectionable element in the negro? It is the object of all education to aid man in becoming a producer as well as a consumer. To enable men and women to make their way in life and contribute to the material wealth of their community or country, to develop the resources of their land, is the mainspring in the work of all our schools and public or private systems of training. From a material point of view we find that one of the great differences—in fact, contrasts—between the North and the South, is a difference of widespread intelligence. Labor, skilled or intelligent, coupled with the impetus arising from capital, will touch the South as with a magnetic hand, and that region with marvelous resources and immeasurable capabilities will blossom as the rose. It is a matter of observation and history that a section or country that seeks to keep its labor-producing class ignorant, keeps itself poor; and the nation or state is subject to education in order to make it a safe guide in the realm of moral obligation. I think it is Dr. Buchner, who says "Treatise on Man": "It is a generally recognized fact, and moreover sufficiently proved by history, that the idea of morality in the general, as in the particular, becomes further and more strongly developed in proportion as culture, intelligence and knowledge of the necessary laws of the common weal increase." The negro's moral condition, against which objection is raised is the result of his training in the peculiar institution. It taught him no moral obligations of the home, for it recognized no home in the civilized of the term; it rather encouraged him to violate the sacred bonds of husband and wife, because, in so doing, he was taught the advancement of interest of his master in adding to the number and value of his human stock for the plantation or the market. He was prompted, under scanty provisions for physical sustenance, to appropriate his master's hog or chicken to his own strength and comfort, on the principle and argument that he was simply improving his master's property. When a woman was made to feel her honor, which is the glory of every true woman, was not her right, but subject to the carnal caprice of a master, it is not strange that an impression thus deepened by centuries of outrage should make her rather lightly regard this honor just after escape from such a school and from under such a system of instruction. It is certainly apparent, in the light of what has already been done for the moral improvement of the negro, that education will undo much of that which slavery has done to him. Hear what Dr. Haygood says: "No theory of universal education entertained by a rational people proposes knowledge as a substitute for virtue, or virtue as a substitute for knowledge. Both are necessary. Without virtue, knowledge is unreliable and dangerous; without knowledge, virtue is blind and impotent." ... "I must say a word in defense," says this same authority, "of the negroes, particularly those living in the Southern States. Considering the antecedents of the race in Africa, in those States before the emancipation and their condition today, the real surprise is that there is so much virtue and purity among them." ... "Above all things," says Dr. Haygood, "let the white people set them better examples." Since progress has already been made in this direction, we are permitted to hope that education will continue its beneficent work in the moral reformation of the people. Education will certainly afford a better knowledge of the duties of the home, a better appreciation of the obligations of the marriage state, a more consistent regard for the rights and the property of others, and a clearer conception of what virtue in womanhood signifies, and, therefore, a more determined purpose and means of defending that honor from the assaults of any r even at the very risk of their lives.

THE GREAT WORK TO BE DONE.

The great work of education among negroes consists in leading them out of the errors which centuries of a debasing servitude fastened upon them, but even when this is done, the negro will not be an embodiment of every moral excellence, but he will at least stand on the same plane of morals with the other representatives of our common and fallen humanity, and whatever is the possibility and hope of one will be the possibility and hope other, so far as education is concerned; for under it, we believe that the negro can be and do what any other race can do, from the tickling of the soil with his hoe and plow, to make it burst forth into life giving fruitage, to the lifting of world upon world upon the lever of his thought, that they may instruct and entertain him as they pass his vision in grandeur in the heavens. But do we find in the negro exclusively all the immorality involved in the solution of the race problem? Not by any means. After the necessary evidence is given which entitles a man to the recognition of his rights, and these rights are still denied, then the one denying them surprising, then, that men brought up in the face of such a system for two hundred and fifty years should be skeptical as to the real manhood of the negro, and hesitate to give dim a place in the one-blood family. The feeling against the Negro, which helps to make our race problem, is called prejudice, and is not without some grounds. For two hundred and fifty years the white man of the South saw only the animal, or mechanical, side of the Negro. Wherever he looked, there was degradation, ignorance, superstition, darkness there, and nothing more, as he thought. The man was a shadowed and concealed by the debasing appetites and destructive and avaricious passions of the animal; therefore the race problem of today is not anomaly it is the natural and logical product of an environment of centuries. I am no pessimist. I do not believe we are approaching a race war in the South. I entertain an impression, which is rapidly deepening into a conviction, that the problem can and will be solved peaceably; but this can only be done by changing the character of the environment which has produced it. It is an unfavorable condition which has given the country a race problem and it will never be solved until we put at work the forces that will give us a changed condition. This does not argue nor imply the removal of the environment, as is suggested by colonization, deportation, or amalgamation, but it does mean a transformation of the same environment.

THE REAL ELEMENT OF POWER IN THE RACE PROBLEM.

What is the great element of power in the race problem? It is opposition to the claims of manhood and constitutional rights as made by the negro or his friends, because it is thought that he is not in all things a man like other men. It is an avowed determination to resist the full exercise of his inalienable and God given rights. It is a premeditated purpose not to give him justice. In some portions of the country this spirit is more violent than in others; but it manifests itself, in one form or another, the land over. Sometime it denies to the man of the negro race the exercise of his elective franchise; refuses to accord him first class accommodations in public highways of travel, on land or sea, when he pays for the same; denies him, however competent and qualified, an opportunity to earn an honest living, simply because he belongs to a different race; and seeks to organize a Southern Education Association, because it is said that the National Educational Association "has some ways that do not at all accord with the conditions of Southern society," or "for

obvious reasons"; and, as one has said, "to be out of smelling
distance of the sable brother." When it is asked, Why this
opposition, this determination, and this premeditated
purpose against the human and constitutional rights of a
man and citizen? we are told, directly and indirectly, that
while there are rare and commendable exceptions, the
race, as such, is ignorant, poverty stricken, and degraded.
Now if ignorance, poverty, and moral degradation are the
grounds of objection against the negro, it is not difficult to
discover that the knotty elements of the race problem are
the intellectual, moral, and material conditions of the negro
race. It is reasonable, therefore, to suppose that if we can find
the means that will change these conditions, we have found
a key to the problem, and gone a great distance toward its
satisfactory solution. Of course none of us would argue that
intelligence, or even education, is a panacea for all the ills
of mankind; for, when educated, a Nero, a Robespierre, a
Benedict Arnold, an absconding State treasurer, or a New
York sneak-thief, would not necessarily be impossibilities.
I do not argue that increased intelligence, or multiplied
facilities for education, will, by some magic spell, transform
the negro into the symmetry, grace, and beauty of a Grecian
embodiment of excellence. It is certainly not my humble task
to attempt to prove that education will, in a day or a decade,
or a century, rid the black man of all the Price Memorial
AME Zion Church, formerly Price Temple, was founded
in 1895 by Warren C. Coleman, a local African-American
businessman and owner/operator of the first black-owned
textile mill, the Coleman Manufacturing Company (1899–
1904), in North Carolina. Coleman and eighteen members
of Zion Hill AME Zion Church became dissatisfied and
left to establish what is now known as Price Memorial,
"the church in the heart of the city for the hearts of the
people." Price Temple grew from a small one-room cottage
built by its gifted members to the present-day structure.
A small parsonage was erected in the early 1900s and was
remodeled in 1944 during the pastorate of Rev. J. H. C.

Blue. The parsonage was torn down in 1960. The present parsonage, located at 52 Chestnut Street, was acquired in the early 1980s. An educational building was erected in 1954 under the administration of Dr. George L. Blackwell, fulfilling the dream of Rev. I. B. Turner, who passed away during his pastorate at Price Memorial. The church's present organizational structure is credited to Rev. S. R. Lomax, who held the longest pastorate from 1957 to 1964.

The sanctuary was refurbished in 1986 with carpet, cushioned pews, a church-wide PA system, and a comfortable conference room. Under the leadership of Dr. Jewett L. Walker, dedicated members and friends donated gifts to this furbishing and building up of the church. Dr. Walker was also instrumental in organizing the first family day in 1987, which has continued annually on the third Sunday in March.

On August 29, 1993, the Family Life Center was dedicated under the pastorate of Rev. Reynard Ruston. Price Memorial's Family Life Center provides a meeting place for community, religious, educational, civic, and social activities.

The sanctuary was refurbished in 1946 under the leadership of Rev. A. A. Speight and in 2010 under the leadership of Rev. J. Ruth Davis. Also in 2010, the sanctuary was fully renovated. The foundation had serious structural damage due to a water-runoff issue combined with a lack of funds for maintenance. The foundation and interior damage was repaired. In the process, the original handmade bricks were discovered. Dilapidated wood in the sanctuary was removed, replaced by Sheetrock, and then painted. This was done under the previous administration. Because of the generosity of the Cannon Foundation, funds received in 2010 were allocated to the much-needed repairs. The receiving of this grant sparked a spirit of giving into our capital campaign. Over $20,000 was added to the building fund and used to pay off the mortgage (approximately $12,000) of the Allen T. Small Family Life Center in June.

In addition to the regular church organizations and class leaders, Price Memorial has added several additional ones: the Leah Peay Historical Guild, which keeps stat records and maintains historical data; the Robert Reid Helpers Sunday School Class, which garners the monetary and spiritual support of interested members; the Fifth Sunday Men's Fellowship, which discusses various issues of importance; and the Reading Library, located in the upper level of the Educational Building, which houses black history information, AME Zion Church literature, and other educational materials.

The first minister was the Reverend J. L. Sides, followed by forty-plus dedicated pastors through the years. Rev. Robert P. Mathis Jr. is serving as the current pastor. We give honor to God for his blessings through these 124 years in the history of the Price Memorial AME Zion Church.

Coleman/Barringer Historical Family Tree and Black History

Daniel Coleman (attorney) Barringers   Frederick Douglass (1819)

William Coleman
(attorney, master)

Roxana Coleman (slave) Rufus (attorney)** Moreau**, Victor (attorney)

Three children from   Thomas (1845)
John Young

One unknown (Joseph   Warren (1849)
Smith)

                                                   Dr. Price passes (1893)
                                                   Price Memorial (1895)
                        (Three wives) Rufus
                        Jr. Osmond
                        Anna, Paul

                                                   Atlanta Conference

                                                   Douglass passes (1895)

                                                   Booker T. Washington
                        Warren passes (1904)
                                                   W. E. B. Du Bois

Former mayors of Concord before war

                                                   NAACP and others

WORDS FROM THE CIVIL WAR

Concordian decodes diary of Confederate Gen. Barringer

"April 1st, 1865. This day the power of the Confederacy was broken."

The writer: The Confederacy's General Rufus Barringer, a native of Cabarrus County.

Before volunteering when the war began in April 1861, Barringer had been a lawyer in Concord.

By war's end, he had risen to general and was an honored prisoner of war, captured by Yankees wearing Confederate uniforms. In federal custody, he met President Lincoln.

A modest if forceful cavalry general, Barringer kept a short diary – April 1, 1865, to Aug. 8, 1865 – covering innumerable war subjects, in choppy sentences with odd abbreviations.

Some 135 years later, another Concordian completed a transcription and revision of the general's diary.

"It was a labor of love," says Jack Foard, who patiently waded through the diary, researching every entry, to produce an inch-thick copy of everything in it – reducing the hundreds of names and addresses of prisoners of war and military officers to the 37 pages of narrative.

The result is a historic boon for us today, providing a rather cryptic mirror of those final apocalyptic days of the war.

Thanks for your massive endeavor, Jack. Now we'll pick up on the general's narrative:

"Yesterday Grant advanced his cavalry to feel our force in the direction of the Five Forks (Virginia, where Barringer's Brigade had been in fierce fighting).

"My Brigade on the extreme right met the enemy – Davis Division – drove it over beyond

A LOOK BACK

Helen Arthur-Cornett

Chamberlain Run – but the Va. Regt. (Virginia regiment) sent to press him was repulsed & we were forced to retire – recrossing the stream.

"In the afternoon I was ordered to drive the enemy from his position. This was met gallantly there by the 1, 2, & 5 Regts.

"The troops crossing the run up to their works in water & under heavy fire. We drove the enemy a mile & a half & then withdrew.

"My loss this day was 170 killed, (including) Col. McNeill, Lt. Col. Shaw, Capt. Dewey, Capt. Coleman, Lt. Lindsay, Lt. Hathaway & Lt. Blair & among the wounded Lt. Col Cowles, Majr. McLeod. Lt. Col. Gaines, Capt. Harris, Capt. Johnson, & others.

"Early this morning the enemy advanced. We held him in check until toward 12 o'clo. when we quietly retired.

"Late in the evening the enemy attacked Pickets Div. (division) at Five Forks completely routing it & all the supporting troops.

"The men rushed panic-stricken along the White Oak Road – through the country.

"My Brig. (brigade) made a noble stand, charged the enemy's cavalry several times with great success & only retired when the Yankee Infantry approached within 200 yards of our left flank.

"We fell back to the South Side Road at Fords – rested till morning.

"My Loss slight in today's fighting.

"April 1. About 10 o'clock the enemy advance from toward Depot, Beales Brigade skirmished with him.

"About 12, heard of the fall of Petersburg. At 1, recd. orders to fall back towards Trinity church. Campt near Namozine CH (church).

"April 3d. Was ordered to cover the road from Namozine CH. to Poplar Spring CH.

"The enemy attacked in large force – drove back my left, & in my effort to get out the 5t Regt. on my right (improperly dismounted by order of Maj. Gen. Fitzhugh Lee) I, with about 100 men, was cut off.

"I took them through the lines & got them out, & was near the Brigade again.

"When I was captured – late in the evening while reconnoitering, by Maj. B.K. Young of Sheridan's Scouts, Lt. Foard, Sgt. Majr. W.R. Webb, Sgt. S.O. Terry & T.F. Brown were captured with me."

Readers may recall Foard – the irrepressible Fred Foard who leaped from a train carrying him to a prison camp in Pennsylvania, who lived for weeks roaming the countryside, outwitting pursuers, trying to return south.

He was an ancestor of today's transcriber, Jack Foard.

"Maj. Young & party," Gen. Barringer's diary continued, "treated us well.

"Taken to Sheridan's H.Qtrs. at my consent near Namozine C.H. reaching there about 10 at night – all paroled & rested well."

More in my next column.

Helen Arthur-Cornett is a writer for Cabarrus Neighbors and a local historian.

Concordian decodes diary of Confederate General Barringer

The Ceremony

Allen T. Small Presiding

"Lift Every Voice and Sing"

The Occasion

Remembering	Judge Clarence Horton
Warren Clay Coleman	Doris Moon Peay
The Ceremony	Bishop Cecil Bishop, senior bishop
	Africa Methodist Episcopal Zion Church
The Unveiling	The Honorable George Liles
	Mayor of Concord, North Carolina
Reflections	Relatives of Warren C. Coleman
Closing Prayer	Rev. Dr. J. P. Henderson, pastor
	Price Memorial AME Zion Church

Biography

Warren Clay Coleman was born in Concord, North Carolina, on March 21, 1849. He was the son of Rufus Clay Barringer, later a confederate general, and Roxana Coleman, a slave owned by David Coleman Sr. of Concord. Prior to her marriage to John F. Young, a household slave and blacksmith, Roxana had two sons with Barringer, Thomas Clay and Warren Clay.

Rufus Clay Barringer was the descendant of French Huguenots who migrated from France to England and Germany during the early seventeenth century. Barringer provided the inspiration and financial assistance to Coleman's early business ventures and his establishment of a cotton mill in Concord.

Coleman worked for the Confederacy during the Civil War, making boots and shoes. His first business was a combination barbershop and cake and candy store. Coleman purchased land in the African-American community later (Coleburg or Logan Neighborhood) and constructed a series of inexpensive wood frame rental houses. Largely through the efforts of Warren C. Coleman, this area south of Corban Avenue and west of Spring Street became Concord's principal African-American residential community. Between the years 1875 and 1904, he developed nearly one hundred rentals and purchased four farms and a substantial number of city lots, many of them on the southwest outskirts of town; Coleman thereby became one of the county's largest property owners, and he was among the most influential black or white citizens.

In October 1896, the local Republican Party Convention elected Warren C. Coleman unanimously as the party candidate for Cabarrus County commissioner; however, he declined. By 1890, Coleman had considerable influence among fellow African-Americans throughout the state of North Carolina as he was considered one of the richest African-Americans in the South.

Coleman was also a staunch supporter of education. He assisted historically black colleges and universities, such as Barber-Scotia

College, Howard University, Livingstone College, and Shaw University. He made contributions to the North Carolina Oxford Orphans' Home and aided in the development of the Coleman School in Wellford, South Carolina.

Coleman's philanthropy, him being a trustee of the Zion Hill African Methodist Episcopal Zion Church in Concord, extended throughout the growth of the African Methodist Episcopal Zion Church in Concord. He provided financial assistance to Zion Hill AME Zion, Rock Hill AME Zion, and Price Memorial AME Zion Church of which he was one of the founders.

However, Warren Clay Coleman's major contribution was the employment opportunities presented via the organization of the Coleman Manufacturing Company—the nation's first black-owned and operated textile factory, located at the current site of Fieldcrest Cannon Plant no. 9 (Main Street and Highway 601 South, renamed Warren C. Coleman Boulevard) in Concord, North Carolina.

In February of 1988, Mr. William Morrison, a city employee, coordinated the effort (as a project of the Cabarrus County chapter of NAACP) to obtain a historical marker commemorating the first black-owned and operated textile firm in the United States. The marker was unveiled in 1988 at the US 601 Bypass.

Warren Clay Coleman bequeathed to the citizens of Cabarrus County an exemplary legacy of inspiration and cultural pride. Warren Clay Coleman was funeralized at Price Memorial AME Zion Church, Concord, North Carolina, on April 4, 1904.

Warren C. Coleman

Steering Committee

Mayor George Liles

Mayor Pro Tem Scott Padgett

Councilman Jim Ramseur

Councilman Allen Small

Judge Clarence Horton

Helen Arthur-Cornett	Doris Moon Peay
Rev. Sam Farina	Annette Privette
Rev. Dr. J. P. Henderson	Alex Rankins / Susan Smith
Brian Hiatt	Rev. Harold O. Robinson
Rev. Todd Hobbie	Ella Mae Small
Connie Kincaid	Alice Steele-Robinson
Robert Mathis	Dr. Harold Winkler

Unveiling Ceremony of the Warren C. Coleman Boulevard

Warren Clay Coleman
1849–1904

Commemorating the owner of the first black-owned
and operated textile mill in the United States

Fire station no. 3 in Concord, North Carolina

Wednesday, March 28, 2001 (1:00 p.m.)

To: Warren C. Coleman Steering Committee Members
From: Annette Privette
Date: 2/26/01

NEXT MEETING: The committee will meet at 4 p.m., March 15, 2001 at Price Memorial A.M.E. Zion Church, 192 Spring St., Concord.

Minutes from February 26, 2001

Councilman Allen Small convened the meeting.

MEMBERS PRESENT:

Rev. Harold Robinson	Linda Fesperman
Doris Peay	Annette Privette
Helen Arthur-Cornett	Robert Mathis
Vickie Weant	Allen Small
Ella Mae Small	Rev. Sam Farina
Alice Steele-Robinson	Rev. Todd Hobbie
Connie Kincaid	Alex Rankin
Jim Ramseur	Mayor George Liles
Scott Padgett	

Linda Fesperman, with the Library, shared historical documents with the committee. These documents included newspaper articles, photocopies of photos of Warren Coleman's house and store sites and a deed of the mill property.

Details of the ceremony were discussed and program participants were finalized.

Everyone was asked to give Annette Privette the names of people who should be invited no later than March 8.

Speakers will be finalized no later than March 3.

Alice Steele-Robinson and Rev. Robinson spoke about the program they have drafted.

Souvenirs for the event will be bookmarkers. These bookmarkers could also be distributed in the schools.

Vickie Weant will coordinate this. Speakers will receive keychains or paperweights as a thank you.

Mayor George Liles thanked the committee for their work on the event.

Connie Kincaid will construct a display of photographs and historical documents, which would be donated to the library. The display would be setup at the fire station for the ceremony. Members of the committee are asked to bring any photos or information on Warren Coleman for the display to the next committee meeting.

A bronze plaque, which may be placed at the site of Mr. Coleman's store, was discussed. Connie Kincaid will ask if the downtown commission could possibly contribute to its cost. The total cost would be approximately $400.

Alice Steele-Robinson will invite the Barber Scotia College choir to perform at the ceremony. The ceremony will be 45 minutes in length.

A photo of the steering committee will be taken at the next committee meeting on March 15. The meeting will begin at 4 p.m. and the photo will be taken at 4:30 p.m.

Dedication Service of the Allen T. Small Family Life Center

Sunday, November 12, 2006
2:00 p.m.

Price Memorial AME Zion Church
Rev. Harold O. Robinson, pastor

Rev. Andrew Bowie Smoke
Presiding elder, Concord District

Bishop George W. C. Walker Sr.
Presiding prelate of the Piedmont Episcopal Area

We WELCOME you on this important
and historic day to pay tribute
in loving memory of the life and works of the late Mr. Allen T. Small.

Today, we dedicate and celebrate the naming of this building the
ALLEN T. SMALL FAMILY LIFE CENTER
as a perpetual memory of his dedication, his sacrifices, and his loyal
services rendered to Price Memorial A.M.E.
Zion Church. He will also
be long remembered for his many contributions to the life of our
community that he faithfully shared and
lived by performing his duties
as an educator and as a city councilman. He was the embodiment of
that Biblical truth that true greatness is found in service.

We are grateful to God for allowing us those wonderful and endearing
moments of working together.

TO GOD BE THE GLORY!

CABARRUS NEIGHBORS   THURSDAY, MAY 3, 2001   3K

Diverse hands work to restore old cemetery

By GAIL SMITH-ARRANTS
Staff Writer

Concord Mayor George Liles and Joycelyn Snyder pull and cut vines at Old Campground Cemetery. Restoration efforts at the overgrown cemetery have brought together a diverse mix of volunteers.

Who's Buried There

These are the names discovered so far of people buried at Old Campground Cemetery in Concord. Included are birth and death dates, where available, and other information found through the research of Laura "Feen" Lawing Smith. Names are listed in general order from the cemetery entrance. At the end are those believed to be buried there whose graves have not yet been located.

Diverse hands work to restore old cemetery.

INDEPENDENT TRIBUNE • www.independenttribune.com **LOCAL** FRIDAY, AUGUST 29, 2014 • **3A**

PREPPING FOR THE FUTURE

Family and friends gathered Saturday to support the 16 students who graduated from McCullough's Active Mentoring Services, which helps students prepare for their SAT's as well as provide role models to offer group mentoring, bringing in mentors from the private sector, churches, the community and parents. Organized by Norman McCullough, officials hope to eventually expand the program into Charlotte and other communities. Students who participated in the class hoped for a wide range of careers, including going into the medical field, having a career in the arts, being a pediatrician, being a physical trainer and other careers. McCullough is already taking registrations for his next class, which will be offered in summer 2015. For more information, email normanmccullough1@aol.com or call 704-787-8242.

MICHAEL RIGA/ABG/INDEPENDENT TRIBUNE

Prepping for the future

Was Warren C. Coleman the Richest African-American in America in 1900?

by Norman J. McCullough Sr. (January 21, 2019)
Source: https://www.independenttribune.com/news/local/was-warren-c-coleman-the-richest-african-american-in-america/article_c315daea-lb56-lle9-8d8f-a7a88b7440c5.html

Was Warren C. Coleman the richest African-American in America in 1900? Some, a very few, would say "yes" and many others, most, would say "no in 1900 or ever."

Other historians have agreed that Coleman was the richest African-American in the South. As an historian working on the life and times of Warren C. Coleman for the past five years, the evidence that I have recently discovered indicates that Coleman was the richest African-American as of 1900. Other African-Americans became millionaires after 1900, but before 1900, no other former African-American slave, was in the position of Warren C. Coleman, given his material wealth and family background. How come no one else is talking about these facts?

The historical record shows, I recently discovered, that Coleman owned property up and down Depot Street (currently Cabarrus Avenue), around Lincoln Street, Spring Street, various parts of "Coleburg" and various lots outside Cabarrus County. His wealth was extensive. His various possessions included imported horses, a grocery store, his own home on Church and Cabarrus Ave., and various properties that generate rental money on a monthly basis.

In addition, the incorporation papers of 1895/1896—for the mill—shows that Coleman was given permission to own over 1,000 square feet of property and his associates were thinking about a mill town where people working in the mill could live, work, have children, eat food, and go to church, given the "Jim Crow" South. It is no wonder that he would build a church (Price Temple) on Spring Street, which would be within walking distance for many of the people working for him. Coleman and many of his professional associates, and several whites, were building what some people would call "black power" or "black enterprise" before it was coined in the 1960s and 1970s.

Clearly before his time, Coleman, when one looks at the incorporation papers 1896, shows the names of some of the most professional black people in North Carolina at the time. People like, Bishop J.W. Hood, Dr. D.J. Sanders, Dr. Lawson Andrew Scruggs, Edward A. Johnson, Esquire, and 16 others too numerous to mention, were making a way where there was no way. They were making a way for former slaves and others living in Concord. Given all of this evidence, one should begin to ask, where did Coleman glean the expertise needed to buy, sell and manage real estate and other assets—as a former slave—to make him a very wealthy man—but put it all in jeopardy—as he decided to build a mill—at great risk?

The answer is, in fact, and without a doubt and with no other explanation, from his "master" William Coleman, an attorney and his biological father, Rufus Barringer, also an attorney. The record indicates, without a doubt that Coleman's biological father assisted him in acquiring real estate in black areas of the town. Like the relationship between President Thomas Jefferson and Sally Hemings, General Rufus Barringer, did not go around with a loud speaker announcing that Coleman was his son.

During the 1890s, when Coleman was seeking money or other resource for his "textile" mill, many people in Concord may have known who Coleman's father was, but his father was spending most of his time in Charlotte and advertising that General Rufus Barringer had a "love" affair in the 1840s with a black slave was not necessarily in his interest.

When one looks at the fact that the 1890s was a time of severe racial strife in North Carolina, it is a wonder that a man like Warren C. Coleman, who was quite wealthy and could live anywhere in the country, would consider doing anything positive in Concord, N.C. Why don't we know more about this man and his times who clearly loved his town?

The historical evidence also shows that Coleman was on the cutting edge of black leadership in 1895 during the Atlanta Exposition in Atlanta, Georgia because of his close relationship with Booker T. Washington. Washington became the leader due to the death of Frederick Douglass, and D. Joseph C. Price. He (Washington) became the leader of black America. In other words, Coleman was in the middle of an historical world wind of a transitional leadership in the black community. Again, how come no one is talking about these facts?

If you are interested in looking and learning more about the facts, and there are many more, come to the Cannon Library on Union Street on Feb. 23 between 1 and 3 p.m.

Mr. Coleman spent a great deal of his time at his store on Union Street. Moreover, on April 27, the Price Memorial AME Zion Church will hold its 2nd Annual W.C. Coleman Day Street Festival between noon and 6 p.m. on Union Street, across from the Old Courthouse. We will continue to celebrate on Sunday, April 28. Your support, to ensure the continued existence of Coleman's church (built own his land, and financed by him) would be greatly appreciated.

Mr. Coleman gave his all for Concord, N.C. Let's show that his legacy will continue to live in his town and will grow in the interest of the citizens, like myself, both black and white. As we begin celebrating another great man, Dr. Martin Luther King, Jr., let us do so with another great man in mind—Warren C. Coleman.

Norman J. McCullough Sr. is a history instructor at Rowan-Cabarrus Community College, and he is also a trustee at Price Memorial. In addition, Norman is writing a book about the life and times of Warren C. Coleman from an inside/black perspective. It should be completed by the end of the year 2019. He can be reached at normanmcculloughl@ aol.com.

The home of Warren and Jane Coleman situated
at 80 East Cabarrus Avenue in Concord

(Photo by Lawson Bond Studio / courtesy of R. C. Stinson)

(1) Gray's New Map of Concord, North Carolina, 1882.
(2) Cabarrus County Register of Deeds Book 34, Page 405.
(3) Cabarrus County Register of Deeds Book 38, Page 508.
(4) Historical Material, Thomas L. Moose.
(5) Ibid.
(6) Ibid.
(7) The Concord Register, June 12, 1880.
(8) Daily Concord Standard, January 23, 1891.

Subject: SAT Prep/Mentoring

For your information, the SAT Prep/Mentoring program will begin again for the third year on June 27, 2015. There are still a few seats for any youth you may want to recommend. As you know, those students who get a high score on the SAT get into a good school and receive scholarship money. Time is of the essence. You can come to 192 Spring St. NW on Wednesday, June 24, 2015 between 5:00 p.m. and 7:00 p.m. or Saturday June 27, 2015 at 10:00 a.m. sharp. For any questions, please call 704.787.8242. Stay well and God bless.

Hello Mr. McCullough This is Robert Mack and I would like to inform you that I have graduated with a 4.0 GPA and am attending Western Carolina University wanting to major in International Studies but still looking at my options because theres more that intrest me than that one particular area. I was wondering if you needed help with tutoring any of the students for your SAT program in particular math.

Thank you Have a Nice Day

Chapter Five

Photos and Other Documents

Celebrating
Warren C. Coleman

Sat. Feb. 23 · 1 pm

Local educator and mentor Norman J. McCullough shares insights on Warren C. Coleman's place in history and his relevance to young people today.

Come find out why McCullough thinks Concord's pioneering African American textile mill owner deserves to be known across the nation.

CABARRUS COUNTY
Public Library System

Cabarrus County Public Library
27 Union Street North
Concord, North Carolina 28025 | 704-920-2050
cabarruscounty.us/departments/library

81

PROCLAMATION
OFFICE OF THE MAYOR

WHEREAS, Warren Clay Coleman (March 28, 1849 – March 31, 1904) was the son of a slave who went on to become one of the most remarkable figures in Cabarrus County history; and

WHEREAS, from 1873 – 1874, he attended Howard University to prepare himself for business opportunities; and

WHEREAS, between 1875 and 1904, Mr. Coleman bought land and constructed wood frame houses, which became a vibrant African American residential community within Concord; and

WHEREAS, he is most famous for starting the nation's first African-American owned and operated textile factory, Coleman Manufacturing Company, which at its peak employed 300 African American workers; and

WHEREAS, Mr. Coleman founded Price Memorial AME Zion Church and was a community leader in Concord; and

WHEREAS, through the humanitarian efforts of Warren C. Coleman, the social, political, economic and educational level of citizens in Cabarrus County was improved.

NOW, THEREFORE, I, William C. Dusch, Mayor, and on behalf of the City Council of the City of Concord, do hereby proclaim February 1, 2018 as

"WARREN C. COLEMAN DAY"

in the City of Concord and encourage citizens to join the community in a day of celebration on Saturday, February 24, 2018.

In witness whereof I have hereunto set my hand and caused this seal to be affixed.

William C. Dusch, Mayor

ATTEST:

In accordance with a proclamation by the City of Concord
and in conjunction with the AME Zion Church

You are invited to be a part of a Historical Day!

WARREN C. COLEMAN DAY

UNION STREET (DOWNTOWN)

SATURDAY, APRIL 27, 2019 — 12:00 NOON UNTIL 6:00 P.M.

Vendors and volunteers are welcome to attend.

Your cooperation is greatly appreciated. Please notify others.

FOR MORE INFORMATION CALL (704) 787-8242 Mr. Norman McCullough, Coordinator

DEDICATION SERVICE
Of The
ALLEN T. SMALLL FAMILY LIFE CENTER

Sunday, November 12, 2006
2:00 P.M.

Price Memorial A.M.E. Zion Church
Reverend Harold O. Robinson, Pastor

Reverend Andrew Bowie Smoke
Presiding Elder, Concord District

Bishop George W. C. Walker, Sr.
Presiding Prelate Piedmont Episcopal Area

Chapter Six

Working with Booker T. Washington

> In our efforts to rise, we may for a while have obstacles
> cast in our pathway, we may be inconvenienced,
> but we can never be defeated in our purpose.
> —Booker T. Washington

Booker T. Washington

As a wealthy powerful Southerner, there should be no surprise that Mr. Coleman would make every effort to have a relationship with Booker T. Washington of Alabama. The record indicates that Coleman's relationship with Washington was not extensive. The record also shows that like Mr. Coleman, Booker T. Washington's father was white, but Washington did not know him. And it was common practice for white men to take advantage of black female slaves then (note the example of President Thomas Jefferson and Sally Hemings). Coleman was seven years older than Washington, and he believed that he was born in 1856. Washington was never sure, and he spent most of his adult life in Alabama. According to Harlan's book, Coleman went with Washington when he (Washington) made his famous speech that propelled him into the leadership of black America. Harlan said, "In the same procession of carriages with Washington were Bishop Wesley J.

Gaines, … and William (Warren) C. Coleman, the N.C. Negro Cotton Manufacturer."[63] Based on my travel to Tuskegee, Alabama, in May 2019, there was no evidence to substantiate that Coleman was in fact alongside Washington on his way to the 1895 Exposition. Coleman was a victim of Jim Crow, a former slave, and his opportunities to grow as a manufacturer were inherently limited. For example, in comparison, ten years before opening the Coleman Mill, Cannon opened his first mill. However, the review of the record at Tuskegee, when I arrived in May 2019, shows that Washington and Coleman had a minor relationship. In other words, Washington knew what Coleman was doing and encouraged him to proceed. Before going into the details of my findings at Tuskegee, which I visited in May 2019, I must say something about Tuskegee University.

Visit to Tuskegee and Livingstone College

I was informed by Mr. Dana Chandler, the person in charge of the archives, that the Tuskegee University had over 180 buildings. This number is a far cry from a shanty and church occupied by the first building available to Washington in 1881. This fact (over 180 buildings) alone was mind-bending. I later learned on their web page that there were sixty-four degree programs, the faculty to student ratio was 13 to 1, and the university was designated a national historic site. The university currently excels in the area of chemical, electrical, and mechanical engineering, which is a far cry from low-level endeavors that many black people criticized Washington for in the early days. The college was founded in 1881, when Coleman was thirty-two years old and working to make a difference in Concord, North Carolina. How did Tuskegee University become such a substantial university? In order to understand it, one needs to look at the people who invested in the university founded by Washington and Lewis Adams and George Campbell. All these men made a difference for America. Difference makers also included Andrew Carnegie, Henry R. Rogers, George Eastman, Julius Rosenwald, Robert C. Ogden, Collis P. Huntington, William H. Baldwin Jr., Anna T. Jeanes, Julius Rosenwald, and many others. The question is, How many students have graduated from 1881 to 2019 (138 years), and what difference are they making in the world? The answer will also be mind-bending and demonstrates, without a doubt, what one man can do to change the world. Unknown to many, Washington also advocated for the end of lynching. However, with the need to accommodate so many whites, his posture was quite different than Ida B. Wells. Wells, as an anti-lynching crusader, will be discussed further in the book. In June 2019, I visited Livingstone College, which is about forty minutes from Concord, North Carolina. Joseph C. Price was its first president; and my church, Price Memorial, was named after him by Coleman. The campus is in reasonable condition; and the City of Salisbury is expanding, building, and making a difference for Rowan County. During this visit, I was also informed that Andrew Carnegie, a man who made a difference for Tuskegee University, also made a difference for Livingstone. His picture is situated in the library in a manner where one could not miss it. The college has sixteen buildings.

Morehouse College, another major HBCU, is a major educational institution; and people come from all over the world to attend it. The school is known for developing Rhodes scholars, and many of its students move on to receive doctorate degrees. As of August 2019, Mr. Chance Barringer, a son of Price Memorial, has been accepted into Morehouse. Chance has six more siblings to follow him. After seeing him accept many gifts from the church, it was clear to me that the church will live on into the future. These children will be able to pick up the torch when I and many of the elders are gone. Praise God.

Howard University is another major institution. Coleman attended Howard in the 1870s. Coleman was a student when O. O. Howard or Edward P. Smith was president.

There are many famous graduates who reads like a who's who of America. People like Ta-Nehisi Coates, Toni Morrison, Thurgood Marshall, Andrew Young, Elijah Cummings, my former boss Mayor David N. Dinkins, and many, many others. Some of the colleges at Howard include the College of Pharmacy, College of Dentistry, School of Business, School of Law, School of Divinity, School of Education, and School of Social Work.

One difference maker for Tuskegee—Andrew Carnegie—gave $20,000 for the construction of a library, with all the work completed by the students. The library consisted of two floors. The second floor consisted of an assembly room where 225 people could fit in one seating. For blacks, Carnegie made a difference. However, while he was giving to blacks, he was giving much more to whites. Carnegie was born in 1835 and died in 1919. Clearly another prime example of white privilege. When African-Americans were operating as slaves, for the most part, and building up the wealth of America, Carnegie was building his empire without restrictions. Carnegie was known as the person who developed the concept of gospel of wealth. Examples of this great wealth, where a small fraction was given to blacks, are the Carnegie Institute of Technology, Carnegie Institution of Washington (DC), Carnegie Mellon University, and the Mellon Institute of Industrial Research. Carnegie also gave millions to institutions in Europe like the universities in Scotland. He also contributed to a fund that later became TIAA-CREF. Carnegie also made it possible for Carnegie Hall to exist. I remember seeing a performance at Carnegie Hall as a teenager, when my family stepped in to save my life; the performer was Paul Robeson.

The history books are clear that Booker T. Washington, after he made his famous 1895 speech, became the leader of black America for a period of time. Years later, historian W. E. B. Du Bois would severely challenge Washington's leadership. However, when one looks at the Washington Papers at Tuskegee, one can see that Washington and Du Bois had a relationship that included Du Bois asking Washington at one point to look out for him in finding another position because he (Du Bois) wanted to leave Wilberforce University at the time.[64] The record also shows that Du Bois was born in 1868, nineteen years after Coleman was born. As such, he had no recollections of slavery or the Civil War. Some of his family members, however, were slaves from the Caribbean. Du Bois, in contrast, went to an integrated high school from Massachusetts as a young man and went to graduate from Harvard with a BA, MA, and PhD. Du Bois also came into contact with T. Fortune, known by both Washington and Coleman.

My experience at Tuskegee was also revealing by showing me that there is a major difference between the investment in the university and the investment in the town. One would say that the town looks like how it looked in the 1950s with the exception of a CVS, fast-food stores, and suitable hotels/motels. It is clear that anyone who graduated from Tuskegee would have to think twice or three times about settling down in the area. What would happen to Tuskegee or Alabama without the legacy of Booker T. Washington? According to a book written by Mr. Harlan, a man who wrote extensively about Washington, Coleman offered Washington the position of president of the mill.[65] Washington, given his current position in 1895 and beyond, turned him down. However, the offer shows that Coleman and Washington had a relationship where Coleman had the ultimate trust and respect for Washington. However, Harlan also makes the point that Washington visited the mill. This point is hard to believe because the records in the Concord Library system, e-systems, shows no record of Mr. Washington going to the mill. If he did make a visit, it was a great secret. Rev. Lee, an adviser for this book, states that Washington did visit the Cabarrus area in the early 1890s. When, how, and where are the questions. There is no documentation about a visit in the Washington Papers, but there is a letter from Coleman to Washington indicating that the mill was being built, and he (Coleman) requested his support.[66]

My visit to Tuskegee revealed that Washington and others thought about building a mill on the campus. The idea was rejected because the feeling was that mill work did not pay enough for blacks working in the mill industry. According to Washington, Coleman had both men and women working in the mill. Washington, for the most part, encouraged Coleman and spoke favorably at his meetings with the Negro Business League. Toward the end of his life, Washington continued to fight discrimination and injustice. One of these fights was related to the film *The Birth of a Nation*. He tried to stop the film or modify it in many different ways so that blacks wouldn't be viewed as subhuman beasts. The film became an overwhelming success despite the grievances of blacks and others.[67]

In my opinion, many people from the North and the South may not fully understand the issues facing Washington. Especially after my visit to Tuskegee and seeing the many accomplishments of the university for myself, I know there are people talking and there are people doing. Like Washington, Warren C. Coleman was a doer. Unfortunately, because blacks do not control the messaging media, we must be very careful about the opinions we formulate, and we should consider the real evidence that exists in the past and in the present. Even though whites clearly assisted Washington, without a doubt, his story falls into the realm of black history. As such, who is going to tell the real story about black people if not black people? While Du Bois and others were speaking and judging from safe places in the North, Washington was speaking and doing in the Deep South. Washington was criticized by many; however, others knew that his conduct must be seen within the context of the times. One of my mentees, who happens to have a PhD, indicated that Washington was a problem. As a former Northerner, I could understand his point. However, as a person now living in the South, my mind has been adjusted. First and foremost, what smacks one about the major differences between the South and the North is the lack of investment for young people in general and black people in particular. This is especially true when young blacks start miles behind the academic starting line. "He (Washington) never said that American minorities would forever forgo the right to vote, to gain a full education or to enjoy the fruits of an integrated society. But he strategically chose not to address the issue in the face of overwhelming white hostility that was a realty of American race relations in the late nineteenth and twentieth centuries."[68] This is the same hostility faced by Martin Luther King Jr., Medgar Evers, and many others throughout the South in the 1950s, '60s, and '70s. Washington went on to make speeches in various parts of the country. He also visited Europe in the early 1900s, which included trips to Holland, Belgium, Paris, and London. The European trip was an activity that the average black man in America at the time could not even imagine. Having others raise the money to make such a trip demonstrates that many people felt that Washington was the leader of black America and a great American leader in spite of the many differences one might find between leaders like Martin Luther King Jr. (one who spoke about the power of love) and Malcolm X (who spoke about the ballot or the bullet).

1895—the Historical Transition

The year 1895 is extremely important because when one looks at the intersection of the lives of Booker T. Washington, Frederick Douglass, and Warren C. Coleman in 1895, we see that Douglass passes away and Washington becomes the leader of black America.

Specifically, before, during, and after the Civil War, the history books are clear that Frederick Douglass was the leader of black America in the nineteenth century. Where does Coleman fit into this transition when one compares his life with Washington and Douglass? Of course, Douglass was the first leader of black America, and Washington came next (given the death of Dr. Joseph C. Price and disregard for Ida B. Wells). Like both of these great leaders, Coleman was also a leader. He was a leader in the field of entrepreneurship. As the leader of the first black textile/manufacturing mill in America and as a real estate mogul, it is my assertion that Coleman should be at a similar level. He is clearly a hidden figure. A historical/hidden figure that most people in America don't know. Before there was a Robert F. Smith (one who paid for the 2019 debt of the class of Morehouse College), there was a Warren C. Coleman. One of the major questions during this period is, What if Price did not die in 1893? Speculation about this question will be discussed further in the book.

Frederick Douglass

Frederick Douglass was born on or around 1818/1819. His work to assist the black community was immeasurable, and his legacy continues to grow as indicated in the recently published book *Frederick Douglas: Prophet of Freedom* by David W. Blight. It is noted there that like so many other slaves born in America, "Douglass lived most of life believing that he had been born in 1817, but a handwritten inventory of slaves, kept by his owner at birth, Aaron Anthony, recorded Frederick Augustus, son of Harriet, Feby [*sic*] 1818."[69] What kind of system would enable people to be placed on the earth and not let them know for sure when they were born? However, if slaves were seen as property, it would not matter—for some people—when a slave was born. In another book *My Bondage and My Freedom*, Douglass makes a point about his birth: "Like other slaves, I cannot tell how old I am. This destitution was among my earliest troubles. I learned when I grew up, that my master—and this is case with masters generally—allowed no questions to be put to him, by which a slave might learn his age."[70]

Douglass, another great man overcoming the legacy of slavery in America, rose to overcome in spite of the horrors of slavery. In the Douglass book, we see the infamous struggle with Douglass and his master (Covey): "Covey at length gave up the contest. Letting me go, he said—puffling and blowing at a great rate—now you scoundrel, go to your work … The fact was, he had not whipped me at all."[71] As I indicated previously, most slaves fathered by white men would most likely not know who their father was. Coleman was one of the exceptions. Regarding the treatment of slaves on the Coleman farm versus the treatment of Douglass, there is no record because Coleman did not write his autobiography, and much of his story has been lost. However, if we look at what happened in Douglass's case, the treatment was unfortunate. "When old master's gestures were violent, ending with a threatening shake of the head, and a sharp snap of his middle finger and thumb, I deemed it wise to keep at a respective distance from him; for, at such times, trifling faults stood, in his his eyes, as momentous offenses; and having both the power and the disposition, the victim had only be near him to catch the punishment, deserved or undeserved."[72] This means that slaveholders were above the law and could do no harm to slaves owned by them. Imagine what this means for black women under the jurisdiction of white men. Douglass, born years before Coleman, as a slave, makes this point during his speech at the Metropolitan AME Church in 1894: "The fate of the republic was at in this crisis of violence. Stop violating the Constitutional amendments, he demanded. Cultivate kindness and humanity, instead of hatred. Cease degrading one group to elevate another." And to white people, he admonished, "Conquer your prejudices." Oh, how that applies today in 2019.[73]

Did Coleman know about or of Douglass? I am certain that he did know about him, especially when he spent one or two years at Howard University. As such, after the death of Dr. Joseph C. Price at thirty-nine years old and after the death of Frederick Douglass, Coleman must have realized that our time on earth is short and the accomplishments and challenges of life must be met as soon as possible. Because Coleman was a young man when Douglass was striving to end slavery, he did not interact with Douglass, and there is no record of an interaction. Douglass was based in the North, and

Coleman operated primarily in Concord, North Carolina. Douglass frequented many locations, and Metropolitan AME Church was one of his favorite spots to speak about his life and other slaves. He was highly critical of the sharecropping system and indicated that it was worse than slavery. Douglass served in Haiti as a consul general; he served from 1877 to 1885. During this same period, it should be noted that Coleman was operating his store, developing his real estate empire, and living his life as a former slave in North Carolina. Toward the end of his life, Douglass gave several speeches about the horror of lynching that affected the black community. He interacted with people like William Tunnell (a good friend), Ida B. Wells, and his wife Helen. Once he passed, Douglass's body remained in the New York City Hall for two hours—an honor also afforded to presidents Lincoln and Ulysses Grant who remained in state in the same location.

However, Coleman did interact with Douglass's next in line, who turned out to be Booker T. Washington. Coleman's interaction with Washington at the Atlanta Exposition in 1895 will be discussed later. The legacy of Booker T. Washington is very important. Washington was the second leader of black America. Like Douglass, Washington did not know who his father was or when he was born. It is assumed to be sometime in 1856, but it is not clear. Also like Coleman, Washington appeared to be ambitious and willing to learn: "In 1872, at the age of sixteen, Washington entered Hampton Normal and Agricultural Institute in Hampton Virginia; it turned out to be one the most important steps of his life."10 Washington later found himself as the leader of Tuskegee Institute, where he was able to excel and become the leader of the country in 1895. Prior to the beginning of the great exposition in Atlanta, Georgia, there was the world's fair, which was held in Chicago in 1893. This was a gathering to celebrate the landing of Christopher Columbus in the new world. The record indicates that blacks like Frederick Douglass were not recognized, and there were complaints. As such, the organizers declared a colored day when black people were allowed to come in for free. However, given the complaints from people like Ida B. Wells and Douglass, one can be certain that the people in Atlanta did not want to make the same mistake.

Atlanta Exposition

The 1895 Cotton States and International Exposition was held at Piedmont Park in Atlanta, Georgia, from September 18, 1895 to December 31, 1895. Going to Atlanta in 1895 was the same year the Price Temple was built. The record indicates that over eight hundred thousand people attended, and the focus was on agriculture and technology. President Grover Cleveland presided over the opening of the exposition. There was a Negro Building, headed by Irvine Garland Penn of Pennsylvania, and a Woman's Building and various other exhibits that were set up to impress people in the nation and others from around the world. The record indicates that the Negro Day at the expo was December 26, 1895, and most blacks must have been proud to demonstrate their abilities thirty years after the end of slavery and the Civil War.11 The record shows that there were 634 gold medals, 444 silver medals, and 495 bronze medals given out to the various exhibits. The number of medals received by blacks is not clear.

When one looks at Washington's autobiography, *Up from Slavery*, his feelings about the prospect of making his famous speech are as follows: "On the morning of September 17, 1895, together with Mrs. Washington and my three children, I started for Atlanta. I felt a good deal as I suppose a man feels when is on the way to the gallows."[74] Washington was another reluctant leader who steps into the breech like Martin Luther King Jr. Taking over the leadership of the black community in the late 1800s was no easy task. According to Washington, one of the achievements was the erection of the Negro Building, and he makes the point that the Negro Building was on par with others in the exposition. Another important consideration was whether a Negro should be a keynote speaker. As silly as this might sound today, having a Negro on the same platform as Southern whites was unusual. Some came to cheer, and others came to see Washington make a fool of himself. Suffice to say, Washington was successful in his efforts to speak about the condition of blacks in America in 1895. This was the same year that Coleman built his church (Price Memorial) and the same year that Coleman's biological father died and the same year that Douglass died. These events, coming together and highlighted in this book, are significant points for most historians to take note of, moving forward into the future. A year later, in 1896, Coleman announced that he was planning to build a mill in Concord, North Carolina. Relative to whites, according to Mr. Horton, the first mill, known as the Lock Mill, was built in 1839 or ten years before Coleman was born.

Washington Becomes the Leader of Black America

In the Norrell book, we see that Timothy Thomas Fortune, the same Thomas Fortune who was at Howard University with Coleman, states, "It looks as if you are our Douglass, Fortune wrote to Booker soon after the Atlanta speech. You are the best equipped of the lot of us to be the single figure ahead of the procession. Fortune was empathic that blacks needed one leader."[75] Again, without the availability of Dr. Price, for Fortune and the black community, the options were limited. Fortune was the editor of the *New York Age*, and he became an advocate for black civil rights. During the 1880s and '90s, even Ida B. Wells was considered, but her gender was an obstacle. Fortune and Washington were also very concerned about how blacks were being portrayed in the media. As such, Fortune advised Washington to do whatever was necessary to convey a more positive image. In many ways, based on the evidence available today and the recent past, Fortune felt that as a Southerner, Washington could not speak directly to the issue of hostile race relations. Given this feeling of compromise, Fortune took a more hard-line position and (while drunk) advocated that blacks kill whites in Wilmington in retribution for the riots that took place in the late 1800s. Today we hear about violence in Chicago, which in most cases is black-on-black crime. In the late 1880s, the violence was related to whites attacking blacks, especially in the area of Brownsville. The number of people killed or injured included thirty blacks and two whites.

Although the name Thomas Fortune is not known or articulated by many, it should be understood that he played a major role in African-American history, and his candle needs to be risen to shine on a man (Fortune) who rose to the occasion. He was a doer. Because of the violence surrounding blacks in the North and the South, Fortune went through several transformations, and his relationship with Washington was difficult to maintain. Looking at the politics of Washington and

Fortune, one can see that due to the violence of whites against blacks, blacks were divided, and Washington's policy of accommodation was under attack by many in the North and many in the South. When Washington was elevated to be the new leader, the record shows that his stance of compromise would have been quite different when compared to Price's. As noted, "In September 1906 five days of frenzied racial violence rocked Atlanta … Washington gave his usual muted response, urging Atlanta's blacks to exercise self-control."[76] Another source indicates that "Price believed that black self-help through education and economic development was their best hope for solving the race problem, and he assured whites that social integration with them was not their goal. But he was less conciliatory than Washington in demanding the civil rights of blacks be upheld."[77] Nonetheless, one could imagine that if Price had become the new leader, his position on many issues would have been different, and Price and Du Bois would have had a similar point of view when it came to resolving many of the issues facing blacks in the early 1900s.

Another article written by Dr. Lenwood Davis indicates that Dr. Price was the de facto leader of black America in the early 1890s: "J.C. Price, as he was sometimes called, became a widely known leader in 1890 when two national conventions, the Afro-American League and National Protective Association elected him as their president. In 1890 he was also selected as one of the 'The Ten Greatest Negroes Who Ever Lived.'"[78] More specifically, Du Bois, a critic of Washington, indicated that the ideas of Washington were inappropriate. In 1903, eight years after Washington's speech, Mr. Du Bois stated that "Washington's willingness to avoid rocking the racial boat, [sic] calling instead for political power, insistence on civil rights and higher education for Negro youth."[79] In addition, according to Norrell, "A more likely successor to Douglass might have been Joseph Charles Price, a preacher and founder of Livingstone College in Salisbury, North Carolina which like Tuskegee was staffed entirely with black faculty. A great orator, Price nationally known among blacks in the 1880's and had led such civil-rights efforts as the Afro-American League and the National Equal Rights Convention, which Booker had not joined, probably because of his economic orientation for black uplift."[80] Another important activity two years before Price died in accordance with Raleigh State Chronicle in 1891 states that Coleman and Price were working together: "In front were chief marshal, James H. Jones and other leading colored men ... Rev. Dr. Price, Warren C. Coleman, the president and John H. Williamson, secretary of the colored fair."[81] It was a major exposition in Raleigh, North Carolina. I am certain that if Price had become the leader of black America, Coleman would have had a more prominent role in the history of America. These two men were close, which is why Coleman decided to enable Price's name to live, like the pyramids in Egypt, for a long, long time. The history of the church shows that without sufficient financial support, the church could have been destroyed. The spirit of Coleman and his God has kept the church alive.

Chapter Seven

Becoming a Manufacturer in Southern Society and Dying for a Cause

Why let the white boys to have all the fun?
—Reginald Lewis

Fighting Jim Crow

After returning from the Atlanta Conference in 1895, Coleman made a decision to open up a manufacturer's mill in Concord, North Carolina. Because blacks were prohibited from working in the white mills operated by Mr. J. W. Cannon and Mr. William R. Odell or any others, clearly, Mr. Coleman, in spite of the obstacles (a noble experiment), decided to make every effort to make it possible for blacks to earn a living and support their families. There were over 150 mills in North Carolina in the nineteenth and twentieth century, and only one was operated and built by blacks. With limited experience, Coleman decided to sacrifice himself and his entire estate. In comparison to Mr. Cannon and Mr. Odell, we see that Coleman was six years older than Odell (1855) and three years older than Cannon (1852). However, even though Coleman was older, he was behind the eight ball because during this time of mill development, both Odell and Cannon were developing as normal young white men. Cannon opened his mill in 1887; and Odell had opened mills in Durham, Greensboro, and Concord. Clearly there was no level playing field, and blacks were not allowed to work in any of these mills except in low-level, menial positions.

World Industrialization

In England, one of the places where the industrial revolution was born and growing, some people reacted in a way that was violent. They were called Luddites, named after a mythical leader they called General Ludd. According to Judge, these same people "were reacting to industrialization, a momentous shift from a rural agrarian economy, in which people lived off the land and made goods by hand, to an urban manufacturing economy. Where goods were made in urban factories by machine."[82] In Europe, and especially England, the industrial revolution had grown and made many people rich. In fact, their concern for this advantage was important, and those in control did everything to keep the technical aspects of the industry secret.

One person who revealed these secrets about the industrial revolution to America was Samuel Slater. According to USHistory.org, Mr. Slater built a factory from memory and transported the information to the United States. As noted, "From these humble beginnings to the time of the Civil War, there were over two million spindles in over 1,200 cotton factories and 1,500 woolen factories in the U.S."[83] Given this information and given the fact that African-Americans were a substantial part of the population in the eighteenth and nineteenth century, to say that Coleman (with his associates) was the first African-American to build a mill is phenomenal. Another important white mill builder was Francis Cabot Lowell, and he built the Boston Manufacturing Company in 1812—eighty-four years before the development of the Coleman Mill. In the South, unlike the North, many of these industrial mills were found in the country; and most, if not all, were operated by only white employees and owned by white men. The industrial revolution was operating in various parts of Europe and later moved to North America and eventually the South. Coleman, especially in his studies at Howard University, must have been alerted to the fact that African-Americans were not in a position to benefit from the new technology. In the South, most of the mills that were developed and operated were in North Carolina, and many of those were in Concord. As such, Coleman and many of his associates were observing that African-Americans were going to have a limited future if they didn't take action to improve their chances of industrial opportunities.

Other Black Mills

In the book by Allen Burgess, we see another mill involving blacks trying to develop in South Carolina: "At least one cotton mill, the Elmwood Manufacturing Company with its control partially in the hands of blacks and its labor force totally so, becomes less than a great success ... It will be recalled the Elmwood Manufacturing Company of Columbia South Carolina, was the cotton mill organized in 1897 by whites with the assistance of blacks."[84] So to say that Elmwood was a black mill is an overstatement. Other attempts to open a mill in Alabama was not successful. In 1910, another black mill opened and was known as the Durham Textile Mill, a much smaller mill compared to Coleman's with about 150 female workers; and it lasted only five years. The Durham Textile Mill's leadership was headed by another black man who was rich and comparatively unsung—John Merrick. Mr. Merrick was known for his business acumen by starting, like Coleman, a business focused on barbering but later also working with the Merrick-Moore Spauling Real Estate Company, Mechanics and Farmers Bank, and North Carolina Mutual Life Insurance Company. His most successful venture was the NC Mutual Life. As such, he was an entrepreneur, business mogul, and philanthropist. Clearly, he must have looked at Coleman as a role model from an overall business perspective. Yet another black mill in Ocala, Florida, was started in 1915. It was known as the Ocala Knitting and Manufacturing Company, and it was observed that many black females saw these new mills as a way to increase their living standards. However, unlike the Coleman Mill, Ocala was focused only on knitting; so to say that Ocala was a black manufacturing mill by design would be inappropriate. In his *The Booker T. Washington Papers*, Harlan also makes the point that instead of

helping Coleman, Washington tried to assist a mill in Dallas, Texas—
New Century Cotton Mill. However, most of the money utilized to
build the mill was given by whites. As such, saying that New Century
Cotton Mill was a black mill is inappropriate.[85]

Additional Examples of White Privilege

Cannon was also a beneficiary of white privilege. For example,
in another article by Helen Arthur (dated Sunday, April 11, 1999),
she states, "His son, Charles A. Cannon, would build on his father's
beginnings, without discrimination, and join the separate plants into a
company whose name would become famous nationwide."[86] Now with
all due respect to Judge Horton, I would add that "worldwide to that
statement, because as I have traveled in other countries, I have found
people abroad to be quite familiar with Cannon sheets and towels."[87]
In comparison to Coleman, who had no children, it is clear that his
history was cut short; but Coleman's legacy remains in the hearts and
souls of black people and white people who helped to build the town to
make it what it is today. Moreover, it must be emphasized that Cannon
benefited from the wealth that was capitalized in the Coleman Mill and
continued to move forward.

Learning from the Atlanta Exposition

Where did Mr. Coleman get the idea that blacks could build and
operate a mill? As noted previously, it is my thesis that in addition to
being the richest black man in America in 1900, Mr. Coleman went to
the Atlanta Conference in 1895 and decided after seeing and possibly
speaking at the Negro Exhibit that a manufacturing mill was feasible
and necessary. Coleman made this decision given the new technology
developing in various parts of the world. As such, in 1896, we see
Coleman making a speech in front of the Old Court House on Union
Street in Concord. Some of the excerpts are as follows: "Please allow
me to call the attention of the public to the fact that movement is on
[sic] foot to erect a cotton mill at Concord to be operated by colored

labor ... Coleman goes on the make the point that African-Americans are looking for an opportunity. The colored citizens of the United States have had no opportunity to utilize their talents along this line."[88] It should be noted that 1895 was the same year that Price Memorial AME Zion was built in Concord, financed primarily by Mr. Coleman, and the same year that his father passed away. Price Memorial remains intact as of today. An attachment to the church named after Councilman Allen T. Small was completed in 2006. (See chapter 5.)

The First Black Mill in America

There were over 150 mills in the state of North Carolina in the late 1800s, but only one was built and operated by African-Americans. The Coleman Mill was the first (see pictures of the mill). This fact alone makes Mr. Coleman and his associates major (hidden) figures in American history. Having a say about the newly developing industrial revolution was very important for African-Americans like Coleman. Coleman saw that his people (even though he was half-white) were being left behind and needed to acquire the new skills that mills were providing for the young and old. In America, during the Coleman years, if you were one-eighth black, you were black and treated accordingly.

The record at the Concord Library also indicates that Coleman wrote to Booker T. Washington on several occasions; however, a reply was not observed. And in the book by Mr. Norrell, he does not indicate that Washington was thinking about Coleman in any meaningful way.[89] It appears that Washington's focus was on the opinions of people like W. E. B. Du Bois and other critics. People like William Hannibal Thomas and William Monroe Trotter were unrelenting in their opposition to the Washington model of racial compromise. Washington (as one of the Southern supervisors), coming from Atlanta, Georgia, would say he had bigger fish to fry.

Given the fact that Concord had so many mills, it is interesting to make a point of their lifestyle. Mill folk lived close to the bone. In the 1910s, kerosene lamps and open fireplaces provided heat. Families drew their water from wells or hydrants shared with neighbors, and almost all households had outdoor toilets. The lifestyle of most white mill workers was bleak, so blacks were even worse. As noted in "The Evolution of Textile Mill Villages" by Bennett M. Judkins and Dorothy Lodge, we see that "the mill owner provided shelter, jobs, medical care and schooling and maintained authority over the private lives of his employees."[90] Most of the mills in the South were located in North Carolina, in places like Alamance, Bellemont, Burlington, Canton, Carolina, Cliffside, Concord, Cooleemee, Mount Holly, and many others. Working and living in a mill town was normal for many people living in North Carolina during the nineteenth century.9 Moreover, in the Chicken Hill, Asheville's newest neighborhood, it is noted that "the spinning room was incredibly hot all the time ... There was very little medical help available [sic] worker ... If you got hurt and could not work, you stayed at home without pay."[91]

When we look at the Coleman Incorporation papers filed in 1896 with the state assembly, we see the following very successful people listed: Bishop J. W. Hood, Isaac H. Smith, Dr. D. J. Sanders, Rev. C. McNeil, Rev. F. G. Ragland, Rev. J. S. Settle, Rev. Elias J. Gregg, Rev. N. I. Bakke, Rev. S. C. Thompson, Mr. John R. Hawkins, Mrs. Polly A. King, Mr. Lawson Andrew Scruggs, Edward A. Johnson, Esq., Mr. L. P. Berry, Mr. Richard B. Fitzgerald, Mr. John C. Dancy, Mr. Marshall J. Corl, Charles Frances Meserve, Mr. Robert McCrae, and Professor S. B. Pride—a total of twenty people, seventeen blacks and three whites, with one female included.[92] The board of directors included John C. Dancy, Rev. S. C. Thompson, Professor S. B. Price, Charles Francis Meserve, Edward A. Johnson, L. P. Berry, Richard B. Fitzgerald, and Robert McCrae. Coleman also associated with whites like John M. Odell and J. W. Cannon and Washington Duke. Many of these people provided financial support. Coleman also met at times with L. D. Coltrane (Concord National Bank), William Smith, and Dr. D. J. Satterfield (president of Scotia Seminary). Another member of the board was Charles F. Meserve (white), who later became the second president of Shaw University.

In other words, Mr. Coleman, by way of his personality and training, was able to bring all these talented men and woman together to make a way for those unable to make a way for themselves. "Another major supporter for the Coleman Mill was Honorable George H. White. Congressman White was the last African-American to serve in Congress until Oscar De Priest in 1928."[93] During the 1897 ceremony to celebrate the building of the mill, we see that wealthy white people were in attendance. Part of the crowd included John M. Odell and J. W. Cannon, and both made speeches in support of the first black textile mill. Coleman was also a farmer who owned horses, cattle, hogs, and melons. Given the historic nature of the mill, in 2016, the mill was put on the National Register of Historic Places in America.

Mr. Richard Burton Fitzgerald of Durham (a major brick master) was the president of the mill. Mr. Coleman was the chief operating officer. Like Coleman, Fitzgerald was from a mixed racial background, and he was also the president of Mechanics and Farmers Bank in Durham, North Carolina. When we look at the many people involved in this high-level operation over thirty years after the Civil War, people like Frederick Douglass, Booker T. Washington, Warren C. Coleman, and many others were clearly making a difference in America in spite of their status as former chattel slaves. Frederick Douglass was a great orator and editor, whereas Washington was an influential educator and fundraiser. On the other hand, Coleman excelled in the area of entrepreneurship. His mark remains in the town of Concord for the world to see, and his legacy will remain in the hearts and minds of people who are willing to fight against the odds.[94] Whether the town of Concord truly wants to preserve the Coleman legacy is a matter for further discussion and review for people in various parts of the country.

When we look at one of the people working with Coleman to assist African-Americans in America, Mr. Fitzgerald was one of the most noteworthy. Mr. Fitzgerald was born in 1843 until he died in 1918. He was born in New Castle County, Delaware, from a mixed-race family. Given his birth, Fitzgerald was six years older than Coleman, so he could have provided the wisdom of an older person and taken charge of the mill accordingly. At the height of his brick-making business, Fitzgerald was able to produce thirty thousand bricks per day. In addition to the Coleman Mill, Fitzgerald provided bricks for the Central Prison in Raleigh, North Carolina; Emmanuel AME Church in Durham, North Carolina; St. Joseph AME Church in Durham; and the Fitzgerald Building in Durham. What happened to Fitzgerald when Coleman passed? Fitzgerald went on continue his brick making business, and he was able to produce thirty thousand per day. In addition, Fitzgerald became involved with a bank (the Mechanics and Farmers Bank), which was able to make a difference in Durham, North Carolina, and other locations. He passed in 1918 and was buried in Durham.

Another great person of color making a difference was John C. Dancy. He was known as a politician, journalist, and educator in North Carolina and Washington, DC. In Mr. Dancy, we see another young man who attended Howard University in 1873. He became the editor of the AME Zion Church's quarterly newspaper, *Star of Zion*, in 1897; and he was later appointed the collector of customs in Wilmington, North Carolina, by four different presidents and the Record of Deeds. He was appointed as the recorder of deeds from 1901 to 1910, so he was pretty occupied once Coleman passed in 1904. Dancy also had relationships and supported white Republicans like John A. Logan and John Sherman. Dancy was born in 1857, which means he was eight years younger than Coleman. He later had five children. He died in 1920 (two years after Fitzgerald) and also became a trustee at Livingstone College.12 Mr. Dancy was also observed, according to Norrell, speaking at a commencement at the Tuskegee Institute in 1896.[95]

The record also shows that Coleman was also given permission to buy and sell all articles made of wood, iron, steel, and tin. He was also able to sell bricks, pipes, tiles, and all kinds of items made of clay, sand, dirt, rock, and stone. In addition, Ms. Arthur (in 1992) makes note of a *Charlotte Observer* article that indicates that the Coleman Cotton Mill was making money.[96] How was this possible? It is possible; if one remembers, his father (Rufus) served at the state level, and his influence must have played a role with the incorporation.

Another great man involved with the mill was Charles Francis Meserve. Meserve was white, but he was closely associated with Shaw University. He attended Colby College in Waterville, Maine, as a young man. He was also awarded an LLD in 1899, while Coleman was on the verge of producing goods at the mill. Why Meserve, coming from the North, became close to African-Americans in the South is not clear. His relationships must be tied to his connection with Shaw University and the fact that he remained president until 1919. The record shows that Shaw is a major institution in the black community.

Another powerful man in the Coleman world was Daniel Jackson Sanders, who served as the first black president of Biddle University from 1891 to 1907. Like Coleman, Sanders was born into slavery. He later earned degrees from Lincoln University and decided to go to England and Scotland to earn money for the university. He returned, like Price, with over $6,000. When one looks at the resources provided to various colleges from Europe, it is clear that Europe did their part in trying to elevate blacks in the nineteenth and twentieth century. Price, Sanders, and Wells received financial assistance from the Europeans. Once Sanders married Fannie Price, he fathered nine children. One of them, Danetta, became a professor at Hunter College, where I graduated in 1973 with a bachelor's degree. Sanders died three years after Coleman in 1907.

As we have seen with Fitzgerald, Dancy, Hood, Scruggs, Sanders, and Meserve, they were men of significance. Why would these men follow this man of limited education but powerful influence? To get these men to follow him is a wonder that one must ask. Who was Warren C. Coleman? Another man of significant influence who followed Coleman was Lawson A. Scruggs. Like Coleman, Scruggs was born into slavery. He was another man who overcame the obstacles of chattel slavery in America. Scruggs became an attending physician at St. Agnes Hospital in Raleigh, North Carolina, after being denied membership in the North Carolina Medical Society. Why? Why would early America deny the existence of men like Scruggs? He clearly had a lot to contribute. What is this cancer that negatively impacts our country? Why is race such a powerful negative that it prevents us from understanding the benefits of some people born in our country every year? The story is the same over and over and over: people rising out of poverty or chattel slaves who are abused or others denied an appropriate role in the country. I pray that one day we will overcome this disease called racism and maximize our true potential as a nation. Given the remedies rendered in the 1960s to ban discrimination, we are at the beginning of the process. Taking one or two steps back would be a tremendous mistake. History should be our teacher.

Additional Black Men of Mark

Of course, as we move into the nineteenth and twentieth century, it is clear that Frederick Douglass's shoulder is one that many black men stood on as they pursued their various endeavors. If Douglass had not fought with Covey, his master, he would have been like millions of other slaves, living the life of a chattel slave of no consequence. Douglass made a great difference during the Civil War by fighting for the lives of African-Americans who decided to fight for the Union and were captured by the Confederates. The Confederates advocated the killing of blacks fighting for the Union. Due to the outrage of Douglass, Lincoln issued a retaliatory order that contained a one-for-one policy. In other words, one Union soldier killed would require that one Confederate soldier would have to die. This order made a difference to resolve the problem of African-Americans soldiers being killed arbitrarily.

After reviewing the book written by Mr. William J. Simmons and reviewing the attendant information, it is clear that black men born during the middle of the nineteenth century were making a difference that was similar to Coleman, but different in many ways.[97] One major difference is that many of the individuals noted were professionally trained in the legal profession and became attorneys. Others were trained as clergy in the AME or AME Zion Church and also attended Howard University or Oberlin College. Many were also former slaves. Those who were former slaves included Hon. Robert Smalls, who was born in 1839; John Wesley Terry, an attorney born in 1846; Hon. George French Ecton, born in 1846; Rev. Augustus Tolton, a Catholic priest born in 1854; Rev. Frank J. Grimké, born in 1850; and Henry Highland Garnet, born in 1845. Joseph C. Price was also born at a time when he might have been a slave, but his father was a slave and his mother was free—unlike Coleman, whose mother was a slave. Coleman's status was based on a rule of the peculiar institution that states that a person born into the world during slavery was given the status of the mother and not the father.

Some of these men were also professionals at Howard University. They included Rev. John B. Reeve (born in 1831) and Prof. James M. Gregory (born in 1845 and later became the dean). Rev. Frank J. Grimké (born in 1850) also participated, like Coleman, in the Civil War as a valet and also went to Howard University. Others also born during the mid-century included Philip H. Murray, Esq., Jeremiah A. Brown, Prof. J. W. Morris (born in 1850 and became the president of Allen University), Hon. Henry Wilkins Chandler (born in 1852 and became a city clerk and alderman in Ocala, Florida), Jeremiah Baltimore (born in 1852), J. R. Clifford, Esq. (born in West Virginia in 1849), Prof. John H. Burris (president of Allen University), Mr. N. H. Ensley of Nashville (born in 1852), Hon. Robert B. Elliott (member of the House of Representatives), Hon. George H. White (who also went to Howard University), Hon. Josiah T. Settle from Tennessee (who served in the legislature), and Prof. William Eve Holmes (who was a scholar in Hebrew, German, and French. Holmes was born in 1856.13

(Simmons) Timothy Thomas Fortune, Esq., was a key leader in the African-American community in the 1890s and made it clear, based on the death of Joseph C. Price, that Booker T. Washington should be the next leader of black America in spite of the pedigree of all the people noted. Why? Did no one else want the position? This is a question that someone else may want to answer. However, after my trip to Tuskegee and looking at the institution, it is understandable that Washington was seen as a very important person in the black community. Coleman, on the other hand, was a professional in an area not represented by any of the black men mentioned. Coleman was an entrepreneur that became very rich by way of his expertise in the field of real estate. Robert Reed Church was another wealthy real estate professional; however, he (Church) became rich during a time when Coleman was passing away. Additional white people who worked with Coleman included Morrison H. Caldwell, W. G. Means, P. B. Means, and others. Coleman was also elected as president of the North Carolina Industrial Association for the improvement of black people in 1888.

Black Women and the Mill

In a recently published PhD dissertation, Kathryn M. Silva Banks makes the point that women were involved in the textile mill business and the Coleman Mill made a major contribution for their work: "Furthermore, the enterprise gave black women from the small town of Concord, N.C. and across the country, a voice in the growing industrial world."98 In addition, Ms. Silva makes it clear that women played a role inside and outside the mill. One in particular, Sarah Dudley Pettey (the wife of an AME Zion bishop), gave her support to the cause of the Coleman Mill. Ms. Petty was at the cornerstone ceremony. Others included Mary Lynch from Livingstone College, Frances Harper (a poet), and Hattie Bomar (a teacher at Scotia Seminary). Who was Sarah Dudley Pettey? Sarah D. Pettey was born after the Civil War, and she was a voice for those who never experienced slavery and learned that education was the key to true liberation. Pettey was born in New Bern, North Carolina, in 1969, twenty years younger than Coleman. She attended a normal school and later graduated from Scotia Seminary in 1883. By 1883, Coleman was buying, selling, and managing real estate in Concord; and he must have become aware of Petty. Her husband became a bishop of the AME Zion Church and began to publish her thoughts about female rights and the like in the *Star of Zion* publication. Pettey was a strong advocate of the mill and felt that the mill was a key to progress for African-Americans, both men and women.[99] Thus, when Coleman arrived at the Atlanta Conference and beyond, he was not only representing himself but also many others aspiring to achieve their goals and ambitions as business people in America. Given Mr. Coleman's achievements, it was no surprise that he was being considered to be a representative of the Cabarrus County Commission in 1896, but he later decided to withdraw his nomination because he wanted to focus on the mill. In addition, after looking at the evidence in Tuskegee, the evidence on file indicates that Washington was under the impression that both men and women worked in the mill.

Child Labor

In addition to men, women, and others working in and outside the mill, it must be understood that children were also employed. It is clear that they were able to do low-labor jobs such as sweeping and keeping the mill clean. In addition, most large mills also had youths who performed the duties of a doffer. Doffers were nimble-fingered young boys or girls who worked in textile factories, removing and replacing bobbins from the spinning frames. And they were a common sight in American mills until 1933, when child labor laws were finally passed, outlawing the use of children under school age. Moreover, in Wikipedia, we see that "doffer in 1887 in a large mill in Cabarrus County, N.C., both boys and girls earned 40 cents a day as doffers."[100] Mr. Nesbit, employed in Cabarrus County and a member of Price Memorial, also indicated that he started working for the Cannon Company at fifteen years of age. Moreover, in another book written by Washington, he mentioned that Coleman hired some two hundred boys and girls at one time. He was an early mentor.

Rufus Barringer Passes Away

In 1895, another major event took place in Coleman's life. Aside from building Price Temple and attending the great 1895 Exposition, Coleman's biological father passed away. In the Sheridan Barringer book, it is noted that before passing, "General Barringer wrote his son, Paul I am glad to say that Dr. Graham has got my case under fair control."[101] In the Barringer book, Rufus bade his family farewell on February 3, 1895. Did this farewell include Roxana, Thomas, or Warren? The book doesn't say. If not, why not? The cause of death was stomach cancer. In further discussion about General Barringer's death, Sheridan makes the point that "the gallery of the annex was reserved for blacks and many attended, remembering Barringer's support for causes benefiting African-Americans."[102] This point is well taken, but did Rufus Barringer and his family do enough? Do white people need to do more to remedy the fruits of their behavior? Warren C. Coleman turned out to be a gigantic historical figure who was at the cutting edge of black leadership in 1895 in spite of his many obstacles. However, what about Thomas? What about Roxana? What about the legacy that remains of chattel slavery? Do we just forget after fifty-plus years of fighting and overcoming Jim Crow? My feelings are mixed. Rufus tried to do something to help his "acknowledged" son. And we are grateful, but do white people need to do more in the immediate and distant future? This is a question that I often tell my students and that they (white youth and others) will have to answer. Over the next ten to thirty years, when I am long gone, this question will remain for the country to answer in one way or another. Some people will continuously call for reparations, while others will seek a wall and/or separation. How did Coleman feel? There is no evidence he felt one way or another. He wanted to help his people in the present. The record is blank, like our solution to the legacy of racism in America.

After I visited the library at the University of North Carolina at Charlotte, I learned from the Barringer papers that he did not mention his black children or his black slave lover. In summary, the papers stated that there were only two members of the Cabarrus Rangers left as of July 7, 1929. The papers also included a daily log showing what Barringer did once he was captured by the Union forces. In addition, there was an article by Billy Arthur indicating that Paul Barringer was an ardent chess player, and he played against Jefferson Davis when he visited. And Paul was living with his uncle Victor. A state marker is located on the spot where Victor's house stood.

Working Against the Odds and Hostile Southern Behavior

On the twenty-second day of February 1897, Coleman was able to acquire the site for the mill. According to Ms. Arthur in her 1992 article, "The mill was completed in 1897, on land bought from M. J. Corl, near the railroad tracks between Wilshire Boulevard and Old Charlotte Road."[103] It should be noted that 1897 was a year after the Supreme Court rendered the *Plessy v. Ferguson* decision 8 to 1. The decision stated that separate but equal was legally acceptable, which cemented the idea of Jim Crow until it was overturned by the *Brown v. Board of Education* decision in 1954, stating that racial separation was inherently unequal. In addition, Ms. Arthur makes this point: "The mill planned for 150 looms and 7,000 spindles produced yarn for the textile trade—slowly at first, but with increasing success." Whether the mill was completed in 1897 or not is in dispute. It appears that a more accurate date for the production of goods would be sometime in 1901. During this period, blacks were required to work and cope with the violence surrounding them in many different places in the country.

Violence against African-Americans in the South was fairly common before and after the Civil War. As I go through the examples of violence in the South, it must be noted that most white people in the South were not part of the violence. However, because many did not object vehemently, it is fair to say that whites benefited from white privilege and the overall mistreatment of blacks in the South and other places. Just like the supporters of Donald Trump, people may not be racist, but their silence is condoning a racist president. Specifically in the book written by Blight, we see this: "Grant refused for too long to intervene in Mississippi, and by the fall some three hundred blacks had been killed in political terror throughout the countryside."[104] This event took place in 1874 and preceded many other events during the same century. During this same period (or 1898), racism was rampant. And an uproar occurred in Concord, North Carolina, when Mr. Hartsell's daughter was allegedly raped by two blacks, Joe Kizer and Tom Johnstone, who were later hanged by a mob of white men in Concord. Were the black men guilty? The record does not say. According to the *Western Sentinel*, Ms. Emma Hartsell's throat was cut from ear to ear. And it said that "Sunday night the crowd broke down the door and got the men … The horror of the incident was documented and would create a chill in any civilized society … the prisoners protested innocence but they were carried about 3 miles from Concord where a tree was found on which [*sic*] were two limbs about three feet apart … the noose was adjusted around each man's neck, the box removed and the bodies dropped." To make this horror more chilling, the article ends by stating that "a few minutes after the drop [*sic*] 100 shots were fired at the dangling bodies, riddling them with bullets … Their bodies were left hanging."[105] How blacks were treated in the South in America at this time was clearly outrageous. According to Mr. Burgess, the killing of the two young black men had a negative impact on the efforts to build the mill in Concord. No other inquiry into this matter has ever been discussed.

Mr. Norrell notes that violence was widespread in response to various forms of Reconstruction: "With the return of the U.S. army to govern much of the South, a coalition of local Unionist, Yankees, and blacks took control of state government. This new challenge provoked more white terrorism: the Ku Klux Klan rode at night to scare blacks and their few white allies into submission, killing them when necessary."[106] Moreover, in 1898, racial tensions were high in Wilmington; and people wearing red shirts killed several blacks and burned several buildings. The impact was tremendous, and it is noted that "some 1,500 black residents of Wilmington fled."[107] The violence in North Carolina was clearly a problem, and many black men reacted to the abuse of black women: "Tell your men that it is no worse for a black man to be intimate with a white women than for a white man to be intimate with a with a colored woman ... Don't think ever that your women will remain pure while you are debauching ours."[108] There was also violence in Texas, South Carolina, and New Orleans; and lynching was common in the South. And it must be understood that in addition to black men, black women were also subjected to this inhuman treatment. The treatment of one black female in Georgia who was pregnant was so cruel that discussing it further is only fit for a horror movie. My stomach turned when I first read about this incident. It was described as follows: "In Valdosta, Georgia, in 1918, after Mary Turner's husband was lynched, she publicly vowed to bring those responsible to justice. Although she was eight months pregnant, a mob seized her, tied her ankles together, and hanged her upside down from a tree. Someone slit her abdomen, and her nearly full-term child fell to the ground. The mob stomped the infant to death. They then set Turner's clothes on fire and shot her. Moreover, the whites in leadership (Vardaman was running for governor of Mississippi) were very clear about their feelings concerning black advancement. Vardaman stated that the Negro was a curse to the nation, a lazy, lying, lustful animal which no conceivable amount of training can transform into a tolerable citizen."[109] The mind can't absorb how people could be so cruel to kill this mother and child. What kind of man—made in the image of God—would kill another human in a manner not suitable for an animal? In fact, many animals are treated much better. However, it must be understood that many Americans still don't believe that blacks are human.

In addition, as noted by Mr. Burgess, "Despite the Wilmington tragedy, and many other dreadful incidents, the installation of the engine, boiler and related equipment continued throughout the fall and early winter. By late December 1898, that portion of the mill's equipment was ready for testing."[110] Moreover, by 1900, we see Mr. Dancy state this in the December issue of the *AME Zion Quarterly Review*: "The mill is finally in operation running on full time with its fair quota of operation and noting that five houses had already been built by the company and that contracts had been let for construction of five more."[111] As the evidence is clear, the mill was under construction in 1896 with the support of the community, as noted previously. However, full operation did not take place until 1901 or 1902. As such, we are talking about four years of construction and four years of actual operation to produce material products. How so many black people were able to come together and build this massive structure that remains visible today is truly historic and remarkable. Like the pyramid in Egypt/Kemet, it must be preserved at all cost. By 1902, the mill was operating at 100 percent or full speed with over one hundred blacks employed and as many as three hundred employed in the mill or in real estate before his death in 1904. Coleman's real estate transactions were a part of the mill's operations.[112]

However, moving upstream in terms of my knowledge of Coleman, the record shows that textiles, in general, were in major decline in the early 1900s; so Coleman's probability for success was very low. The record also shows that another Duke assisted Mr. Coleman. Ben Duke provided help by giving Coleman $10,000 minus $1,200.[113] Once the mill was no longer viable on or about 1904, Duke foreclosed and later sold the mill to Mr. Cannon. Because Mr. Coleman's activity was at such a high level, historian W. E. B. Du Bois spoke about Coleman's achievements while he (Du Bois) was in Europe in the 1900s. Du Bois wanted the world to know that African-Americans were capable of the highest level of activity in a world becoming more and more industrial. At about the same time (1902), one of the employees of the mill, George Kiser, was killed while sleeping on one of the railroad tracks.[114] Whether Mr. Kiser was buried at the Old Camp Ground Cemetery or not is not clear. Today, the Kiser name is well represented in the Price Memorial 2019 souvenir booklet, and the Kiser emblem was submitted by Ms. Regenia Ann Kiser in 2019.[115] Looking back at the Kiser genealogy would be a very interesting project for the City of Concord.

In addition to his many achievements as a real estate mogul and manufacturer, Coleman was given the capacity to become a magistrate (justice of the peace), whereby he possessed a number of law books (maybe from his father or William Coleman). However, because of his color and other technicalities, including his obligation to the mill, he was not able to continue in this role. What else did Coleman do to benefit the white community? As noted, Mr. Duke and Mr. Cannon were able to acquire a major industrial facility (plant no. 9) for little or no money—relatively speaking. Mr. Clarence E. Horton Jr., in his

"History and Background of City of Concord: A Bicentennial Sketch," noted, "Inspired by the success of Odell and Cannon, an enterprising black business man named Warren C. Coleman launched what one biographer called a 'noble experiment' by building a textile plant in Concord to be operated by only African-American employees."[116] After his untimely death, the plant became part of the Cannon business. My only point about the Horton assertion is, if Coleman did not go to the Atlanta Exposition, would he have been inspired to think that African-Americans were capable of working at a high level, as historian W. E. B. Du Bois bragged about during his trip to Paris in Europe? I would assert that much more of the inspiration, given the 1896 timeframe, must be given to the 1895 Exposition. For African-Americans, looking at what white people are doing is quite different than blacks watching what black people are doing. Imagine if the tables were turned and white people (in the minority) were supposed to do what black people were doing. I am certain that Mr. Horton meant well, but without a book like mine, knowing much about the men outlined in this book would not be information lifted above the bush.

Clearly, having a diverse workplace, community, etc., is important. Diversity has been a code word for many years, which means that blacks and others should be included. Other black men and women who also became famous business people include Alonzo Herndon of Atlanta; H. A. Loveless of Montgomery, Alabama; Ms. Maggie Lena Walker of Richmond, who became one of the richest black women in America in the twentieth century; and John Dabney, another wealthy black man from Richmond, Virginia, who also became wealthy due to real estate. However, the most well-known millionaire in the early twentieth century was Madam C. Walker. Her time in the sun began "in 1905 (one year after the death of Coleman) with the $1.50, she developed a formula to nourish and enrich the hair of black women."[117]

Wealth Generated by the Mill

What happened to the wealth generated by the men who built the mill? According to the record, with the death of Coleman and no other appropriate leader or heir to take over, the wealth was transferred to someone else. Who? Mr. Duke or Mr. Cannon? This was a clear transfer of wealth from black men to white men. This transfer is another example of institutional racism or, at minimum, a difference in treatment, which remains in effect as of today. Others might say the wealth disappeared because the Coleman Mill went bankrupt; but as I argue in an *Independent Tribune* article, as of 1900, Coleman was the richest black man in America.[118] What happened to the wealth generated by this man and his associates? Some of his wealth must be attributed to his white father and master who taught him to function in a world where legal training, otherwise unavailable to other slaves, was important. At my former university (Teachers College, Columbia University), it is known as human capital. Coleman was awash in human capital. Cannon, after the mill went bankrupt, clearly benefited from the structure and whatever remained in the mill. Was there an accounting? Once Coleman passed away, Cannon continued to expand his business with very little visible or viable benefit to the black community. This is not to say that the Cannon Foundation has not provided resources to the Logan area, but what was given is a fraction of what was built. Other than the very small amounts that are given to some black churches and others, the Cannon Foundation could do much more to break the cycle of poverty in blacks' areas like Logan. What about factoring in leadership scholarships and making certain that these students have the resources needed to succeed? We need leadership that can challenge the school board members, commissioners, etc. Some people would agree, and others would be afraid out of their minds. With no or very few blacks in a leadership position, the position of whites over blacks and others remains intact and without challenge.

Remember, many blacks could not work in high-level positions for Cannon or any other mill owner until the late '40s and '50s. They were victims of racial discrimination until Jim Crow started to the break down, and the civil rights movement was making it clear that racial discrimination must be declared illegal. If it could be proved that racial discrimination was the reason Coleman was not able to proceed, would someone or some organization be liable? This is not reparations, as some people have called for. This issue is about recapturing the wealth that was generated by black men, with some help from whites, and returning it to the black community. It would appear that doing so would be fair and in the interest of the community. There are ancestors related to Mr. Coleman still around. What about Thomas and his children? What about Roxana's children? Should they be compensated? Having someone look into this matter may prove to be very interesting, especially if we are talking about the difference of treatment based on race and color.

To add injury to injustice, during a seminar at the Cannon Library in Concord on February 23, 2019, the issue of discrimination was discussed further. Were blacks who had contributed greatly to the textile industry in the form of the Coleman Mill considered for employment in the beginning of the twentieth century? The answer, when one looks at the work of Timothy J. Michin, is it was only in a limited manner. Michin notes, "The South's largest industry, textile manufacturing underwent major changes in the racial composition of its work force. The exclusion of African-Americans from textile production jobs— which had pervaded the industry since the 19th century ended in the 1960's and 1970's filling production positions that had previously been occupied by whites only."[119] This means that even though blacks made a major contribution to the industry, they were still not allowed to reap many of the benefits, relatively speaking. The lawsuits were extensive. Michin further says, "African-Americans wrote countless detailed letters to the EEOC documenting discrimination in the mills—these anguished notes led to lawsuits against all of the nations major textile firms like Cone Mills, Burlington Industries and Cannon Mills, among others."[39] Given the overt discrimination against African-American males and females and the obvious contribution of the community at the Coleman Mill, considering legal action by appropriate organizations could be an option in the future. However, when one interviews some of the African-Americans who were employed at plant no. 9 (the Coleman Mill) and other plants as part of the Cannon business enterprise, but only in-low level jobs, Mr. Blakeney stated that he was employed as a truck driver who traveled to many of the plants and he was employed for about twenty years.[40] To say that African-Americans were not employed in mills that were built by African-Americans is not correct. Whether they were given top-level positions, especially in management, is another matter. Another member of Price Memorial indicated that blacks were employed, especially in manual labor positions, to handle cotton and other heavy loads that whites did not want to do. The same person made the point that once the civil rights laws were passed, blacks were employed in all levels of the mill. Another old-timer was Mr. John Nesbit. Nesbit was born in Concord, and he had two girls. Nesbit was still alive when I spoke to him in March 2019. Although his memory was not good, he indicated that he worked for Cannon for over fifty years in plant 1 and 6. Mr. Nesbit is also a lifelong member of Gilmore Chapel (an AME Zion Church), and his history has been preserved in this book for future generations. Mr. Nesbit asserts that blacks were employed at various mills, including plant no. 9 (Coleman's Mill), and he was made a foreman for many years in various locations. Nesbit indicated that "once segregation was eliminated, he was treated very well by the Cannon family." However, like everywhere in the South, blacks were the victims of segregation on a daily basis regarding bathrooms, eating facilities, etc., until outlawed in the 1960s. Overall, Mr. Nesbit stated that his time spent with the Cannon business was one of respect, and his ability to retire with dignity was due partly because of his time with the Cannon business.[41] Another example of progress in the 1960s includes the hiring of Corine Cannon in 1963. She was met with fierce resistance from whites who did not want to give blacks anything in light of their (blacks) contribution to society. At this time, people remained segregated, but Ms. Cannon's arrival indicated a change, and more blacks were hired and served as managers into the future.[42]

Another Wealthy Black Man

Another wealthy black man who became rich at the beginning of the twenty-first century was Robert Reed Church. Like Coleman, Reed's father was white and he knew who his father was. Church was never legally accepted by his father, but he did teach him about the steamboat business. After recovering from a gunshot wound, Church became the owner of a salon, hotel, restaurant, park, auditorium, and several commercial buildings, including a bank on Beal Street. The record indicates that he was a millionaire, but his wealth was generated after 1900. Robert R. Church also became famous because his daughter— Mary Church Terrell—was one of the early supporters of the NAACP and spoke out with many others about the brutality and discrimination faced by African-Americans in the early 1900s. Beal Street also became a famous spot for music lovers and others who wanted to enjoy the South after the Civil War. Given the history of Mr. Church, it is clear that Coleman was the richest black man in America just before 1900. Coleman was rich due to his material wealth and his family affiliation of attorneys on both the Coleman side and the Barringer side of his family.

Other Black Entrepreneurs

As noted previously, Coleman's leadership in the black community is in the realm of entrepreneurship. If nothing else, he was a businessman, and his primary business before building the mill was real estate. Was Coleman a millionaire? Because the record is not fully assessed, I would say that if Coleman was not a millionaire in 1900, he was a very rich man who put his entire estate on the line to acquire the mill and make it operational for poorly educated African-Americans. Other wealthy black people around the same time or before included Mary Ellen Pleasant, William A. Leidesdorff, Robert Reed Church, and Madam C. J. Walker. Others included James Forten, Amanda America Dickson, Paul Cuffee, and Bridget Mason. Some of these people did not want to reveal their wealth because of the discrimination that was evident in the eighteenth and nineteenth century in America, depending on their location. Although Ms. Walker, unlike others, was not afraid to make it clear that she was a wealthy person; and she wanted people to know that she worked hard to acquire her fortune while others may have inherited their wealth when people passed. Again, Coleman made his wealth in the world of real estate and business. Putting forth the resources to build the mill was merely the icing on the cake, and he was clearly not working as a normal black professional in the nineteenth century.

Recently, African-Americans like Oprah Winfrey, Beyoncé, Jay-Z, Robert F. Smith, Michael Jordan, Sean Combs, Tiger Woods, Robert L. Johnson, Magic Johnson, Sheila Johnson, and Tyler Perry are enjoying the liberties of becoming rich in a country where whites have hundreds of times the number of rich people when compared to blacks. All these people have to be thankful to people like Frederick Douglass, Booker

T. Washington, Warren C. Coleman, Ida B. Wells, and many others too numerous to mention. Are current rich black people working on an even playing field fifty-plus years after Jim Crow? The answer to this question remains to be seen, as the wealth in America for African-Americans grows or may remain the same in the future. Looking at the recent events surrounding Mr. Robert F. Smith and Morehouse College, it is clear that some African-Americans are stepping up to the plate by paying off the college debts of all the graduates of the 2019 class. While others, with the devil in their heart, are allegedly trying to sexually satisfy themselves and at the same damage the college—unfortunate. Imagine the impact that these young people will have in America to truly have an impact like Mr. Smith.

Reginald Lewis

Another man in the world of black billionaires was Reginald Lewis. Lewis is another man who has not been advertised or discussed freely in the media market. Most Americans, like the legacy of Coleman, are unaware of Mr. Lewis. Why? Lewis graduated from Harvard Law School. As such, he was an intellectual in the same vein as Paul Robeson. Lewis's ultimate achievement was the acquisition of Beatrice Foods—a billion-dollar company. However, Lewis died, like Coleman, before his time at fifty. Lewis practiced law for fifteen years and started the TLC Group, a financial, and would pass away at the height of his achievement in his home.

Coleman was a man who attempted to do everything he could to assist African-American people. The record is clear: "In the year of 1904 North Carolina had three hundred mills employing 50,000 employees. All of the cotton mills in the State employed white labor except the Coleman Manufacturing Company of the Cabarrus County. This mill was owned, managed, and operated by black people."44 "Dying for this cause is something that many black people may not fully understand. Coleman put his fortune and his body on the line. Because he was a black man trying to uplift his people, he paid the price of ultimate rejection. Warren Coleman's desire to return from his position of Secretary and Treasurer of the Coleman Manufacturing

Company on the first day of January of the year 1904 was not granted at the sixth annual stockholder meeting."45 He was doing this because the mill could not get insurance due to his race.

If one wanted to feel less than a man, this event would have been the worse. To say that Mr. Coleman's skin would have been so thick to withstand this humiliation is beyond belief. Could you say he was heartbroken? Yes! Could you say he was disappointed? Yes. If we don't find specific medical information showing why he died, I would argue that some of the previous factors mentioned must have played a role. However, additional research revealed that Coleman suffered a skin disease known as erysipelas46; and because of this condition, Coleman would often miss meetings in 1901 and 1902. When one looks at the record, Mr. Coleman felt an obligation to do everything possible to assist his people in the Jim Crow South in spite of the odds. He wanted to be like Moses trying to do whatever was possible to assist his people. He wanted to take them out of bondage to the promised land.

Also noted in Mr. Krieger's book was, "During the afternoon of Wednesday, 30 March 1904, Concord lawyer W. G. Means was suddenly called to the bedside of Warren Coleman who had become critically ill. Coleman was incoherent and unable to sign a hastily drawn will."47 Why did Coleman die? It appears he did not have a long-drawn-out illness. Even though his skin disease may have been a factor, without specific evidence, my theory is Warren C. Coleman died because he was stressed beyond belief and he was humiliated to the point where his body could not take it anymore. I know specifically what stress can do to a person, especially a black man in America.

Chapter Eight

The Naming of Highway 601 and Rediscovering the Mill

His life was gentle, the elements so mixed
In him that nature might stand up and say
To the world. This was a man.
                                        —Clarence Horton

Black Influence on Fashion Industry

As noted by my wife, Darnelle, after working forty-five years in the fashion industry, the Coleman products must have landed in New York City. Darnelle worked for fashion houses known as Teal Trainer, James Daugherty, Harve Bernard, and others. She eventually opened her own business, Djohn Inc., and a showroom on Seventh Avenue, which was later known as Fashion Avenue. Although Darnelle was working in the late 1980s and 1990s, Coleman's impact on the fashion industry in the early 1900s must have been noteworthy—from a black perspective. Darnelle also recalls an experience where a representative from Cannon Industry was selling fabrics to her and others in the 1970s. Further research in this regard would be interesting by researching the overall impact of blacks in the fashion industry from 1901 to 2001.

A Legacy Renewed

Sometime before 2001, some people in the Concord, North Carolina, community realized that Warren C. Coleman was not being acknowledged in an appropriate manner. Councilman Allen T. Small was one of those people. The documentation indicates that many of the people who were involved were committed to taking the necessary action to show that Coleman was, although a former slave, a man of great value to the Concord community (also see Warren C. Coleman Steering Committee paperwork on page). Like Cannon, Odell, and Stonewall Jackson (all these men have buildings named after them), Coleman should be appropriately remembered by blacks and whites alike. There were several annual celebrations in 2001 and 2002. Some of the people included Ms. Doris M. Peay, William Morrison, Leah Peay, Mr. and Mrs. James C. Sullivan, Mrs. Alice Steel Robinson, Mrs. Shirley E. Phifer, and Mr. Arthur Cornett. At the dedication in 2001, several historians were noted, including Mr. Clarence Horton and J. K. Rouse; and about two hundred people were at the marker, as reported by the *Independent Tribune*. The marker is located at 35, 23.092 N 80, 35.414 W.[120] Others on the marker committee prior to 2001 included William Morrison, Joan C. Hambric, Viola Barret, Robert Mathis, Betty Eddleman, William Evans, Doris Peay, and Clyde Thompson.

I had an opportunity to interview Ms. Barrett briefly in June 2019. I told Ms. Barret that her name comes up frequently in the history of Concord. She indicated that she was not born in Concord but has lived here since the 1950s and remembers the Logan School. Regarding the marker on Union Street, the record shows that many of Coleman's relatives were present. They included Sadie Daniel Lawring, Laura Lawring Smith, Mazella Young Steele, Michael Smith, and Michael Steel. All these people and their relatives should be proud to know that Warren C. Coleman, in spite of the many challenges and obstacles of being black in America, did everything he could to uplift and assist the black community. He put his entire estate on the line without a lot of assistance from people in the white community. Like Dr. Price, Dr. Sanders, and Ida B. Wells, Coleman may have made more success if he appealed to the sensibilities of the people in Europe for additional funds.

Hon. Allen T. Small

After speaking with Mrs. Allen T. Small, I convinced her that a portion of the book should be devoted to Allen. He made a difference in Concord by his work on the city council and his work with Price Memorial Church. Plus Allen's name is on the overpass that a person rides over approaching Barber-Scotia College. Who was Allen Small? According to a record delivered by Ms. Small, coupled with an interview, the following can be said:

Allen was born on November 17, 1932 in Pittsboro, North Carolina. Mr. Small's parents were John A. Small and Rev. Roxie Small. Ella Mae and Allen met in the library of NC A&T in the fall of 1952 and married in 1956 at the Mount Pisgah AME Church in Hickory, North Carolina. They had two children, Allen Small Jr. and Allan Tory Small. Small served on the Concord Council for nine years, and his favorite food was fried chicken. Allen served in the army and served in the ROTC at A&T. As part of his duties on the Concord City Council, he visited Washington, DC, for the National League of Cities Congressional Conference. Allen's awards were quite numerous. He received the Nehemiah Award and Warren Coleman Award for his leadership and service to the Price Memorial AME Zion Church; the Omega Man of the Year, Distinguished President Award Optimist International; Focus Leadership Award, Focus on Leadership Organization of Charlotte, Meritorious Community Mental Health Services in Cabarrus County, the Piedmont areas. Moreover, Small received the Order of the Long Leaf Pine from the State of North Carolina, and he was the last principal of the Logan High School before it was closed due the Supreme Court ruling regarding *Brown v. Board of Education*.

Small did his part in making sure the Coleman legacy was celebrated in 2001 and 2002. The record on file indicates that on or about 2003, the Price Memorial and the community ceased to continue the Coleman celebration. Nonetheless, as God would have it, 2015 was a time of renewal and a reawaking of the great Coleman spirit. Why didn't our young people know about this great man? Young people in the Logan community and nearby could benefit from this knowledge. To know that the richest black man in America in 1900 was born, bred, and died in Concord, North Carolina, would be very significant for the community—both black and white. Why is it hidden like so many other African-American figures? Could it be a form of racism that continues up until this day?

As I continued to move up the learning curve, approaching the beginning of the top, it became clear that gaining access to the mill developed by Mr. Coleman and many others was important. After learning that the current mill owner, Mr. Bill Bryant, was amiable to a tour of the facility (second and third floor), we were informed that the basement floor was not available but that it was the same size and length of the second and third floor. The members of the church and others in the community, including several white people, became excited that such a historic visit could begin in 2015. There were about ten members of the Coleman committee, and they agreed that having a bus so that people could relax and take a tour to Coleman's many possessions would be a great historic event. The event was recorded for the world to see in the *Independent Tribune* by Michael Knox (dated April 19, 2015). He stated that "from meager beginnings, he [Coleman] rose to become the wealthiest black man in North Carolina by the 1890s. Coleman is most famous for starting Coleman Manufacturing Company, the nation's first textile factory owned and operated by African-Americans, in 1897."[121]

On April 4, 2015, the tour started in the chapel of the Price Memorial Church. Those in the chapel were informed that the chapel was financed primarily by Mr. Coleman and that Rev. Sides was the first pastor. At about 12:30 p.m., about twenty-five people gathered and later boarded the bus. My son, Norman John McCullough Jr., was on the first bus. I later learned that one of Barringer's white relatives, Francis Barringer Medlin, was also on the bus. She asserted that she was proud to know that Warren did so much to help black people. The bus moved from the Church Street along Union Street (where Coleman had his store) and moved up Cabarrus Avenue to Church Street, passing the Fifth Third Bank (where his house was located) and moving down Cabarrus to Old Charlotte Road to Route 601 and later arriving at the mill. There is a sign at the front of the second floor indicating that the mill was built in 1896. Once in the mill, the participants went directly into the second floor. Moving into the second floor, we saw a wall on the left (several pine posts were going up to the ceiling, over sixteen feet tall). We were informed that the three floors were exactly the same. We later moved to the right. Once we moved right, it was clear that the wall on the other end of the mill was not visible due to the length of the maple floor. After we moved down to the right (walking about five minutes), the wall at the other end became visible. Some of the participants also saw black markings on the floor, which indicated where the machines were previously located for various purposes on the second and third floor. One could just imagine black men operating highly technical machines at the turn of the nineteenth century. As one would say, "Hands that picked cotton were now joining in the industrial age to make a way for young people in the South. Some of the participants, once leaving the mill, also saw railroad tracks in the rear of the building where the product was loaded for distances in the North or South."[122]

Walking around the mill to the front the building, one could witness the massive size of the building and comprehend that Warren C. Coleman and his associates had truly accomplished a great historical feat. Especially when one understands that thirty years earlier, several of these men were chattel slaves in America unlike their white counterparts who were free to live and take advantage of the American dream. During the time when the mill was fully operational, clearly the men would take the finished products and move them to the rear and load them on to trains so that products could be sent to market. A very clear example of black capitalism was on display for many to celebrate or fear. However, did the world care? Or were they afraid of the competition? The products from the mill, based on these facts, could have been found in other parts of America and even other parts of the world.

Old Camp Ground Cemetery

After feeling the aura of the many aspects of the mill and feeling the pride that only black people (and maybe some white relatives) could feel given Coleman's accomplishments, I and other members of the church loaded the buses and moved to visit his seventeen-acre cemetery known as the Old Camp Ground Cemetery (OCGC). It is next to the MLK monument near the roundabout. It is a holy place holding the remains of over two hundred black people. Upon arriving at the cemetery, it was clear that the cemetery was not in good shape. In other words, some of the participants indicated to me that someone needs to clean up the cemetery. Unfortunately, this is an ongoing issue; and as of the publication of this book, the cemetery remains in very poor shape. In spite of the poor condition, several of the participants, including several youths, planted American flags on the graves. The flags were planted on some the graves of visible veterans, who are as follows:

PFC William Torrence
Pvt. William Luther Johnson
PFC Wader Roger
Pvt. James Davis
Pvt. Caldwell Smith
Pvt. Leach Smith
Pvt. Richard Moore
Sgt. Charles Wallace
Cpl. David Johnson
Pvt. John Howie
Pvt. Tim L. Boger
Sgt. Wesley Thomas Steele
Pvt. Hazelkia Steele
PFC Archie William
Pvt. Robey Holbrook
Pvt. Mack Harris
Sgt. Herbert Gibson
PFC Arthur G. William

These men who fought for and served America deserve better; and it is my hope that publishing their names in this book will give them a better place to rest. And it is clear that those responsible have decided, for some unknown reason, that these people resting in this place (OCGC) need to remain as third-class citizens and continued victims of racial discrimination, undeserving of a proper place to rest. John Price, another local resident who was interested in the history of the cemetery, was visible as noted in the *Independent Tribune*: "John Price at a tombstone in the Campground off Cabarrus Avenue in

Concord. Much of the cemetery was overgrown when this picture was taken in July 2016."[123] Fortunately, there are people like Kimberly Killer; she made a YouTube video of the cemetery on September 18, 2016. At that time, the condition was somewhat reasonable. As of June 2019, the condition is horrible and an utter disgrace. After feeling the sadness of the cemetery, the bus returned to the church; and the people were able to visit the vendors (including NaSha, an Afrocentric artist and designer; Sandra Smiling, a soap vendor; and others) located in the Allen T. Small Family Center to learn more about the Coleman Estate and his life and times. Regarding cemeteries in Cabarrus/Concord, there is another article by Helen Arthur in 1999 that indicated that the historic Phifer Cemetery may not survive, given the experience of the McClure Cemetery and the Harris Family Cemetery.3 Thus, many cemeteries in Concord, both white and black, are not treated with much reverence. However, the number of white cemeteries underserved are far less than the black cemeteries.

Chapter Nine

Moving into the Future and Concluding Statements

There is not a liberal America and a conservative
America—there is only the United States of America.
— Barack Obama

Future Endeavors and Mentoring

President Obama became the nation's leader because of his vision about
our country that is now (as of 2017) witnessing an age-old test of unity.
It would be great if we were unified. Yes, we are the United States of
America. However, this proposition of unity was tested previously by
war (in 1861); and over six hundred thousand people lost their lives.
Unity came at a very high price. Some people would say that we are
still fighting that war. Some whites don't want lose their past privilege
or their legacy of white supremacy. When will it end, and when can we
truly say that we are united? Only God knows.

Moving into the future is contingent on the young people from the
community keeping the story of Warren C. Coleman and others alive.
In this regard, as indicated previously, McCullough's Active Mentoring
Service Inc. (MAMS) has provided group mentoring for students

from the community between 2013 and 2019. Specifically in 2014 and 2016, the students that were provided the SAT prep/mentoring included Nishawn Milak Anderson, Bryana S. Ardrey, Destanie A. Black, Joshua Ford, Olivia Gadd, Isaiah Nurse, Robert Mack, Coreth Perez, Tnia P. Phifer, Alex Rodriquez, Jorge A. Rodriquez, Onesha R. Sanders, Shianece E. Sanders, Jaden St. John, and Kaja S. Thompson. Many of these students have gone on to college and other secondary programs (see article dated August 29, 2014). I recently heard from Ms. Coreth Perez wherein she said she graduated with a bachelor's from UNC and wanted to help me in future activities. I was so happy to hear from her. In addition, I feel privileged that my education and experience has enabled me to affect these young people in a positive way. This is especially true when you consider my background as a teenager living in the Alfred E. Smith public houses. For those who say that model cities, the GI Bill, and other similar programs don't work, have them look at my life. Paying for college and others can make a difference. Moreover, in 2016, another group was able to receive SAT mentoring/prep from me and other people in the community. The students were as follows: Geoffrey Wayne Cunningham, Kylie Donovan, Odis J. Gadson, Stedman C. Graham, Jamin Glenn, Brenda Graves, Danielle Hillie, Kenan Haywood, Brianna J. Mahoney, Tnia Pearl Phifer (attended several years) Carter R. Thomas, Taylor Walton, and Nayia Wilson. Mentoring, given the blight that exists in many African-American communities, is an activity that many professionals use to reach back to communities in need of assistance. In 2019, I was able to mentor three students in five consecutive days. They were Journe Richards, Immanual A. Smith, and Isaiah Smith. Immanual, based on his behavior, was able to demonstrate a clear advantage in math; and if guided properly, he should be able to make a major impact on the world in the future. As a good friend of mine, Mark Fant, Esq., would say, "That is what I am talking about." May he rest in peace.

The 100 Black Men of America has taken the lead in regard to mentoring in America and various other parts of the world. This was documented in my book *The Dream*, which was written to assist those who might feel uncomfortable with one-on-one mentoring. Group mentoring is different from the mentoring in Thomas W. Dortch's *The Miracles of Mentoring*. During my experience in working with parents (about eighty in Concord), I found that there are different types. Some are not interested because they don't know any better, and their children will suffer because of their lack of interest. There are those who may be poor but understand that education is critical, and they will do anything and everything to see that their children are educated to the fullest extent possible. For this group, mentoring is important, and they will take advantage of any viable program. There are also some who know that their children will benefit from a good education, but they are afraid that their children will grow financially and leave them behind, so they don't make a maximum effort to assist one or more of their children. And there are some, not many, who want to know that their child is mingling with the right group of students. These parents are the same as those who refuse to do anything to look back. Prof. William J. Wilson has made this point on numerous occasions that some professional blacks have done nothing to reach back and help those who are left behind in poverty-stricken areas. As such, there will always be a black underclass because generation after generation, like in the projects where I lived, young people don't see any role models so that they can aspire to do better. They only know and do what they see. This final point is why I wrote *The Dream*.

Dortch makes the point that one must be willing to make the commitment: "Time is a major concern in one-on-one mentoring. As I have mentioned before, you have to be prepared to commit a few hours every week or every other week."[124] In my opinion, one-on-one mentoring is risky. Another consideration is teaching a young person the difference between right and wrong. Who knows what is right or wrong? What is right for one person may not be right for another. Another important consideration for one-on-one mentoring is setting boundaries. "Sometimes, mentoring requires tough love. You have to be willing to say no, to correct, to ask hard questions, and to speak unpleasant truths."[125] Because of these complexities and possible problems that may come up, I would recommend group mentoring. This is especially true if a group or an organization does not feel comfortable with one mentor working with one mentee. This issue is major especially when one believes that a mentor may be attracted to the program for an inappropriate reason.

In my case of mentoring in the town of Concord, North Carolina, it never dawned on me that I would not only mentor (teaching, informing, assisting) the youth but also mentor a whole town. My good friend Dennis Rowe, walking with me since 2014 and before, recently talked about our different mentoring programs—mine operating in Concord, and his in Charlotte. We both agreed that our programs were operating out of churches and that churches could do more to support mentoring for our young people. However, having trusted members perform to do the work of the Lord may mean they are not trusted or maybe the church is programmed to do other things. If the programming is not working, why not focus on something that will ensure the churches' existence in the future by focusing on an activity targeting and meeting the needs of our youth and their families? Having students do well on standardized test while trying to select a college is in the interest of African-American families. Over the years of my mentoring services in New York City; East Orange, New Jersey; the Poconos; and Concord, North Carolina, the following people made a difference: my brothers at the 100 Black Men, Robert Eden of the Poconos, Mr. Amos McClorey, Mrs. Ella Mae Small, Dr. L. Davis, Mr. Dennis Rowe, Officer McCullough of the Concord Police Department, Rev. Johnny McClure, Rev. Robert Mathis, Mr. Thomas Taylor, Mr. Horace Stainback, and many others who were able to witness the work of Warren C. Coleman in full bloom.

All the students identified in this book were given basic information about Warren C. Coleman and the role he played in the Concord community—he was mentoring in a different form. In addition, on February 23, 2019, as part of a black history program at the Cannon Library in Concord, I held a seminar for people in the community, including some of my mentees, my students at Rowan-Cabarrus Community College, relatives of Barringer, and others. Ironically, the Cannon Library was named after Mr. Cannon, and there is an Odell school. But there is no school or other structure for Mr. Coleman. Why? Don't we want our young people to know that Mr. Coleman made a major contribution to the town of Concord? Is a highway (601) that no one really thinks about enough? Is it a beginning, not an end? Maybe someone on the school board would take up the challenge and encourage our students to visit or attend a building dedicated to the memory of Warren C. Coleman/Barringer. Would young black men benefit from the knowledge that a man like Coleman was able to achieve things in spite of the odds? Or is it more appropriate for them to know more about blacks who are incarcerated in the legal justice system? That system is clearly delineated in the book *The New Jim Crow*. Ms. Alexander makes this point: "Republican strategist Ken Philips is often credited for offering the most influential argument in favor of a race-based strategy for Republican political dominance in the South."[126] In addition, Alexander articulates that once arrested, there is a lockdown. "Once arrested, one's chances of ever being truly free of the system, often to the vanishing point." Moreover, according to Ms. Alexander, there is a lifetime term for legalized discrimination: "If they are branded felons by the time they reach the age of twenty-one (as many of them are), they are subject to legalized discrimination for their entire adult lives."[127] Was the fact that Coleman was a former slave (a felon), with a white master and a white father, a factor for third-class citizenship? Would he have been more successful if he were born white or free and his name was Warren C. Barringer? When are we going to face our truth that close to 350 years of slavery and Jim Crow must be addressed in a way that says it (slavery) was beyond evil and that the violence that followed is still having an impact on the black community? The violence that is happening today with the police is also having an effect. Many blacks have been able to overcome this. However, thousands were/have not, and the waste is something that America will pay for in the future. As they say, "Pay me now or pay me later." Paying later is very, very expensive.

Lost History

During discussions with faculty members of my college (RCCC), we often spoke about the need to record history because without it, it (the history) can be lost and never recovered. A clear example of this situation is trying to locate the farm (or area) where Coleman lived with his mother, brother, master, and stepfather. Like his homes, where he lived with his wife, on Church Street and Depot Street, those in control decided to tear down his homes in both locations because it was perceived to be not valuable. Why? Could it be that black history was not considered significant? Could it have been saved? The answer is obvious, especially when one sees that the homes of Mr. Cannon and Mr. Odell were preserved and other buildings exist in their names. It was not in the interest of the town of Concord at that time to save the home of a former slave. It would have been wonderful to see the home and land that produced such a powerful individual in our history—a black man who was born a slave in America and who achieved a lot in spite of the many obstacles in his way. What about Roxana or Thomas and many others who involuntarily supported the Confederacy? What is history if not a documentation of what happened in America and other parts of the world? Other towns and cities have decided to embrace black history. It is time for Concord to do the same.

After recently speaking to Rev. Donald Anthony of Grace Lutheran Church, I was informed that, like the Old Camp Ground Cemetery, there is a neglected Lutheran cemetery near the new jailhouse on Corban Street. It is clear that the town of Concord and others have seen fit to neglect the black cemeteries in the town. Why? Is it a reflection of how people today feel about blacks in general now and in the past? How people take care of cemeteries says a lot about the attitude of the people, both black and white. During the time of Jim Crow, blacks were treated as third-class citizens. It appears that this attitude remains in the way that black cemeteries are treated. Why? I pray that this attitude will change and people in authority will take the necessary steps to correct this situation. After reviewing the Lutheran cemetery again, I found the gravestone of one person. The growth of trees, weeds, etc., was so great that I could only find one gravestone. I was afraid that there may be snakes, insects, etc. The name was Pleasant Miller, who died in 1903, one year before the death of Coleman. Pleasant Miller was a person and a child of God, and yet his resting place is a disgrace. Why? Mr. Miller must have known Coleman, and both of them are in a resting place where no one seems to care. It is almost like they did not exist. The worst of it is that there are other nearby graves at the Lutheran cemetery where the grass has been cut and there are Confederate flags on several grave stones. The Confederate part of the cemetery looked very presentable. The name Bost stood out. Why are these white remains treated better than those people who were black? Preserving the white cemetery while the black portion is neglected has got to say something about those who are living today, both white and black. People in charge have money to do so many things. Why not devote a fraction of it to those who made a difference for us all? No answer is not acceptable. We must do something to remedy this situation, or do we want to just allow the remains to just wash away and let that behavior speak to the spirits where we all us must go in the near or distant future? The City of Concord must do something! It is time for Concord to understand that before one can move forward into the future, one must heal the wounds of the past by acknowledging the injustices that remain as part of our political DNA. Naming a building in the name of Warren C. Coleman with nationwide publicity would be a good start, and cleaning up all viable black cemeteries would be next.

Recently, the name was proposed for a new high school. One of the board members stated, "Having a highway is enough." According to some other high-level officials, getting the highway dedicated to Coleman, who made a difference, was very difficult. Why? The Stonewall Jackson building, built without too much of a hassle, is another example of how some people feel about buildings named for those cherished for all the world to see. When will the contributions of African-Americans in Concord be truly celebrated? Mr. Allen was one man, but there were many others like Richard Fitzgerald and John Dancy.

History Found

In early September 2019, while writing this book, after hearing and reading about Warren C. Coleman, a resident called me and indicated that she was aware of the whereabouts of the cornerstone of the Coleman Mill. She indicated that it has been sitting in her yard for the past four years. This person, who had an impact on history, also sent an email with a picture of the stone. It was carved "Coleman Manufacturing Co. Built 1897." How the stone found itself in this person's yard remains a mystery. The main point is that an important part of American history has been found, and like the history of black men in America involved in the industrial revolution, it is important. Like people in the American Revolution, we must never forget those who made a way for America and African-Americans in particular. This stone is empirical evidence (see picture on page), along with the mill itself, that black men were capable of working at the highest level of technology at the time. Although this (the stone) exists, the person currently in possession of it has stated that her family is claiming ownership and they (her and her family) plan to hold it with no further discussion.

Another major assertion made by this book is that in 1895, Coleman was on the cutting edge of black leadership at the time. Clearly, Coleman was a very rich man; and he wanted Booker T. Washington, the new leader of black America, to acknowledge him. My visit to Tuskegee showed that the university is well-preserved, but the town of Tuskegee is in bad shape. Booker T. Washington—with the death of Frederick Douglass in 1895, the death of Dr. Joseph C. Price in 1893, and the unwillingness to consider a woman (Ida B. Wells)—became the leader of black America.

Warren C. Coleman, at great sacrifice, wanted to become a manufacturer to assist his people. He did not need more money. He had no previous experience in the area of manufacturing. So his heart was in the right place; but his body, I am certain, could not handle the stress. Most whites and blacks in the South were on the bottom of the economic system after the Civil War; however, blacks, on the other hand, were on the bottom of the bottom. Most blacks were illiterate and uneducated. Coleman must have seen that working in the fields or farms was no longer plausible; and he saw that blacks, not given the opportunity to acquire industrial skills, would have their prospects for a productive future go from slim to none. However, without the appropriate expertise and funding needed to succeed, Coleman's challenge was overwhelming. The machinery he acquired was old and worn, but he decided to move ahead in view of the violence and the like.

Mr. Coleman knew that what he was doing in Concord would reverberate throughout the country and the world. Having it take 115 years after his death to have his light ignited to its brightest point must be credited to our God. A God who made a way for all of us, a way out of no way. Unlike other manufacturers, Coleman had no children, so there was no one able to take on the mantle, and his wife was illiterate. If he had a son or daughter who could follow his path, we might have had a continuation of the Coleman Mill in the hands of African-Americans. When we look at the Coleman record, on May 28, 1904, we see an attorney by the name of E. A. Johnson who wanted to keep the mill in the hands of African-Americans. He was not successful. Dr. Price, on the other hand, had several children to carry on his legacy. If Coleman's half-brother would have assisted him, the Coleman legacy may still be more visible. Names like Morrison, Cannon, Odell, Phifer, Hartsell, Barringer, Means, etc., are spoken today on a regular basis in Concord; and there is a woman by the name of Wilma Means who continues to make a difference for our youth. There are at least seven young black people whose surname is Barringer (under the age of eighteen) who regularly attend Price Memorial. In light of this fact and in light of the scrooge of racism and Jim Crow, how could any African-American become successful in America shortly after the Civil War in the South? Many people would say that racism is a major crisis for our country, and plans to eradicate it are needed. Most young African-Americans in the 1900s and even today, 2019, have a harder time finding appropriate employment. Getting into a career path that would give them (young African-American men) a lucrative lifestyle is very difficult in the South. According to Councilman Ella Mae Small, the lack of an appropriate opportunity is why so many of our youth move North or to other parts of the country and never return. Her husband, Allen T. Small, must have felt the same way. Making lukewarm efforts to recruit African-Americans is not enough. Conducting affirmative activities to make sure African-American are included in the pipeline for various jobs is important in Concord. The backlash could be fierce, but people must be made to understand that five or ten years of affirmative activities would be a remedy for close to 350 years of injustice. Conducting a study to ascertain the human capital that was developed in Concord and is benefiting other places would also be interesting. Institutional racism is real and must be eradicated whenever possible. Some people in the Concord community are beginning to look at this (institutional racism) and the cost that is severely and negatively impacting the community and the region.

Lack of opportunity is not as prevalent in the North. In the North, the opportunities for advancement are better for blacks and others seeking greater mobility into the middle class and above. Not finding an appropriate career or lucrative lifestyle would apply to those male and female with a bachelor's and master's degree. Looking at my life is evidence that poor people in the North have a better chance of success when compared to poor people in the South. Having a free college education for all NYC residents in the early twenty-first century made a difference for me and many others. The last and most important point about this book is the fact that blacks and whites, by way of the abuses of slavery, have many relatives that no one wants to talk about. In the Coleman case, like in the family of President Thomas Jefferson and Sally Hemings, people need to come together to share their common history. The legacy of the Civil War battles remains in the air; but human beings, if they desire, can overcome these differences to seek a common heritage going into the future. A heritage that our children will have to live with and face in the near and distant future so that true change can take place. Like the subject of climate change, our children have to bear the burden of our waste and greed and other activities that may doom our planet in the next one hundred years or so. There is no question that slavery was evil, and there is no excuse that can be offered for its existence in America for close to 250 years. Furthermore, Jim Crow was also a stain on our country. In order to remedy and make the country whole, for close to 350 years of injustice, it will be important to continue to look back historically. Looking back is important, but making significant and systematic change will also need to take place. Ensuring that our youth receive an appropriate education, in light of the previous injustices, is extremely important in discussing a resolution. The evidence is clear that black children and white children in Concord are never effectively given the information contained in this book. Why? When you look at the many black universities that people developed after the Civil War, what else do black people have to do? Black people can't do the job needed to resolve the problem by themselves. It must be a unified effort so that our country can move forward without having to go back to the dark days of the Civil War. Again, some people would say that the cold (sometimes hot) war is still going on. Just look at the headlines of young white men trying to kill (mostly black and Hispanic) as many people as possible.

Annual Street Fair

As of February 2018, Price Memorial, in collaboration with the City of Concord, decided to hold an annual street fair from noon to 6:00 p.m. for the first time on Union Street to honor Coleman. Union Street is where Mr. Coleman ran his business. In 2018, fifteen vendors selling various items were able to carry on the spirit of Coleman and let the world know that his legacy remains alive for the youth and others to see. Mr. Rodney and Michael Smith, relatives of Coleman on the John Young side of the family, were also present and took pictures to celebrate the recognition of Coleman and many of the other people supporting him at the turn of the century. Another street fair took place on April 27, 2019. There were three locations where people could celebrate the lives of Coleman and many others. People were located at the church on Union Street, and a 3:00 p.m. prayer vigil was held at the mill. Having this annual event, which is a fundraiser for the church, will ensure that the legacy of Coleman and other people in Concord will continue for years to come. Those who were involved in the April 27, 2019, street fair included my wife (Darnelle McCullough), several members of the church, vendors like Nasha and Sandra Smiling, Arica Rucker, Patricia Coleman, Vanessa Thomas, Denis Butler, Horace Stainback, Celeste Caldwell, Mr. and Mrs. Stocks, Alishia McDaniel, Tia, Dr. Steven Cathcart of RCCC, and Lady Angentque from South Carolina. My brother-in-law, Ed Lawson, and my good friend Dennis Rowe also made donations.4 Another street fair is scheduled for 2020 (see the picture advertising the event on page).

Juneteenth 2019

In view of Coleman Day in Concord in April 2018 and 2019, black leaders of the Concord community decided to celebrate what is known as Juneteenth in the black community. This is a celebration for African-Americans when in Texas in June 19, 1865, black slaves were informed that they were free. This news was significant because in fact, blacks were already free when General Lee surrendered in April 9, 1865, or even before due to the Emancipation Proclamation. However, the news did not travel to Texas until June 19, 1865. Prior to 1865, it should be noted that due to the Civil War, white slave owners were pushing black slaves into Texas. According to Gates's *100 Amazing Facts about the Negro*, more than 150,000 slaves were forced to make the trek to Texas, and blacks were not informed about their freedom until June. Otherwise, celebrating the date often meant that former slaves were beaten or hanged right after 1865 and beyond. How black people were treated is a stain that America has to live with and remedy as soon as possible.

Although blacks have been celebrating this Juneteenth for years in many neighborhoods, I remember my first attendance in Montclair, New Jersey, in the late 1880s. Given the uniqueness of the celebration, the majority population would prefer to celebrate the Fourth of July and ignore the event that affected African-Americans. In Concord, the first Juneteenth event was held at the Marvin Caldwell Park in the Logan community on June 29, 2019. Among the people presenting a program to the community was myself, Mr. Gary Mumford (a drummer), and Ms. Robin Whitehust (a financial adviser). I was able to outline the history of the area and make it clear that prior to Logan, the area was called Coleburg. Several others included Amos McClorey (president of the NAACP) and others. There were African drummers, entertainment, and light refreshments. The leadership also included Terence and Betty Stocks, Rev. Donald Anthony, Rev. Alex Porter, Cherie Jzar, Jean Caldwell, Zenobia Nelson, Rodney Noelle, Nwani, Rodney Smith, Noelle Scott, Greg Havelock, and A. J. Clark. I pray that this program will continue in the future to help uplift the blacks living in the Logan/Coleburg community. Having this event take place on an annual basis is important to the community, both black and white.

Mentoring/Seminars

As I mentioned previously, my mentoring program, McCullough's Active Mentoring Services (MAMS), has been providing the mentoring program with Coleman in mind since 2013 in Concord. Looking to our future, nurturing and developing the young people of our community is extremely important, and I am hopeful that his spirit will carry on in me and many others. Coleman and many of his associates laid the foundation, and we must continue to build on their legacy so that African-Americans and others can understand what it takes to be successful in America in spite of the odds. From 2013 until 2019, several people acted as mentors for the students in attendance. They included Amos McClorey, Mrs. Ella Mae Small, Ms. Marsha Collins, Ms. Nancy Livingston, Dr. Lasheta David, Ms. Cleola Davis, Mr. Thomas Taylor, Rev. Johnny McClure, Rev. Robert Mathis, Officer McCullough of the Concord Police Department, and many others.

From 2015 until 2019, I held several black history seminars discussing Coleman and many of the other men outlined in this book. The purpose of the seminar is to provide basic information to residents and others about history that is not well-known or discussed in private or public settings. Specifically, on February 22, 2017, a historical seminar and art show were held at Price Memorial by members of the congregation and NaSa. We discussed the life and times of Warren C. Coleman, Dr. Joseph C. Price, Rev. Frank Logan, Bishop J. W. Hood, and Rev. David James Koontz (a Lutheran pastor). At the end of the seminar, prior to the art show, the following was noted:

- All these men were born before the Civil War.
- All were known by some, but most were unsung to the larger community.
- All focused on education and especially the need for higher education while others (not listed) felt that higher education was not necessary.
- Those born before 1850—Hood, Coleman, and Koontz—had less education, while Price and Logan were college-educated.
- Hood was a mentor for both Price and Coleman. Price was born in 1854 and died in 1893. Price died when he was only thirty-nine years old. His legacy is clearly visible in Cabarrus and Rowan County, North Carolina. MLK was also thirty-nine years old when he was murdered.
- Thomas Fortune, a close friend of Booker T. Washington, was also born into slavery and decided (with the death of Price) that Washington should be the leader of black America.

I also conducted seminars at the various historical societies in Mount Pleasant, North Carolina and Concord, North Carolina. At both, representatives of the Coleman and Barringer family were present and expressed their interest in learning more about the history of their various families. Specifically, a relative of the Coleman/Smith family, Rodney Smith, indicated that he was very happy that the history of his family was being documented and disseminated to others. Kim Barringer (a relative of Rufus Barringer and his mother), who attended the bus tour in 2015 and the seminar in Concord, stated that he wanted to learn as much as possible. As noted previously, one of Barringer's family member tried to locate the whereabouts of the Coleman/Barringer farm without success.

Recommendations for Church Development

Considering the current situation with the AME Zion Church, with regard to attracting younger members and surviving financially and given my seven-year experience with Price Memorial, I would recommend the following in the memory of Warren C. Coleman, not necessarily in hierarchical order:

- One, in the South (many of these points may also apply to churches in the North) and on a church-by-church basis, churches should focus heavily on offering services. If the membership is low, this may be difficult, but not impossible. A small thing like calling members on the phone can work. Many members, I am certain, would appreciate a call from the pastor or another high-level member once or twice in a two-to-three-month period. For example, "Hi, I am calling to see how you and family are doing. If they are feeling good, we would love to see you in church." It doesn't cost much, but it can make a big difference if people are thinking about watching a game or going to church. Recently, some have said, "If you don't come to church, you don't know what is going on." While some people are unable to come to church every Sunday.

- Another service that would be good is, if applicable, making certain that young people under five can have a separate place to be within the church. Depending on the number, someone can take note of their birthdays and try to provide something for the young people. I am certain that their parents will appreciate this gesture. In some churches, this would not be applicable because none of the current members have made any children recently. However, they may have grandchildren that could benefit from this.
- Vacation Bible School is another service that works well in most churches, assuming one has three or four people willing to do the work that is required to prepare religious education for several days. Some churches have joined with two or three other churches to make the sessions cost-effective. It is also important, given how society is changing to incorporate other pertinent issues like technology and others.
- Another important feature, which is not necessarily a service, is making certain that people in the congregation know what is going on with the church. Having too many secrets is not a good formula for growth. A meeting once a month with the entire congregation would be a good idea.
- There are many other things that should be considered that don't require a lot of money. Taking time for the church is important. Having an empty church or affiliate building for four, five, or six days a week is not appropriate if the church wants to maintain or grow its membership.
- Overall, I would recommend that the church comes together and comes up with additional points that would not cost a lot but would require some time from the pastor and the membership. Why am I making these recommendations? First, I love the church, and I see these recommendations as part of my calling. In addition, as I look at the people in this book and the sacrifices they made to develop the churches, schools, etc., it is imperative that people (talented tenth and all) today continue to make a difference for the young people who will follow in our footsteps.

- As an educator, I have set up SAT prep/mentoring programs, seminars, etc., to make certain that our young people have a chance and the knowledge needed to survive in a hostile country for African-Americans. The church continues to have a role to play, and the church must do everything to remain relevant. If not, many churches will have to close. Having two, three, or four members is not viable for any church. Warren C. Coleman, J. W. Hood, Rev. Sides, and many others would roll over in their graves if what they have built goes to waste or disappears. We must do everything possible to regroup and revitalize as many black churches as possible. In many communities, the black church is really the only true institution that we can say belongs to black people, in spite of our feelings about how it may or may not be operated.

A Six-Year Summary

Those in secondary school utilizing this book as part of their curriculum may want to look at these points first and later go to the specific area in the book to get more details.

After working and living in Concord for the past six years and researching/writing this book, I learned the following:

- Rufus Barringer (confederate general) and Roxana Coleman (slave) had a love affair; they were the parents of Warren C. Coleman and Thomas Coleman (slaves). Rufus had four other white children with three white women.
- General J. R. Jones of the Confederacy also had relationships with two black females, had several children, and also fought in the Battle of Chancellorsville (whether Barringer was there at the same time requires more research). Barringer was wounded several times during the war. The record also shows that two other generals may have been Coleman. They included generals Lawrence S. Baker or Laurence O'Brien.
- General Barringer was related to Stonewall Jackson and General D. H. Hill by way of his marriage to Eugenia Morrison.

- Coleman, Washington, and Douglass were former slaves fathered by white men. Coleman knew who his father was, but the others did not. Rufus Barringer was determined to be Warren's father due to the sale of property originally owned by Rufus Barringer.
- The historical record indicates that blacks owned slaves for various reasons in America. Black slaveholders were amazing, but not unlike the Africans who captured blacks and sold them to whites in Africa and shipped them to the New World.
- Coleman's stepfather was another slave who lived on the Coleman farm prior to the Civil War.
- The John Street United Methodist Church in New York City is where the AME Zion Church was born. People like Rev. James Varick, Mr. Peter Williams, and others made their mark on John Street. The AME Church, on the other hand, was founded in Philadelphia under the leadership of Richard Allen.
- Coleman, Washington, and Douglass were interconnected in 1895, and they all played a role in the historical intersection of leadership in black America in 1895. Washington was an educator and fundraiser, Douglass was an abolitionist and orator, and Coleman was a rich entrepreneur and real estate developer who hoped to develop a mill town.
- Coleman's store on Union Street was burned three times in the 1880s.
- Mr. Hiram Rhodes Revels, born in North Carolina in 1827, was the first African-American senator in 1870 or twenty-one years after the birth of Coleman. Revels was born free from a mixed-race family, which means his mother was free. Coleman's mother was a slave.
- Dr. Joseph C. Price was born in 1854; he died in 1893. He was only thirty-nine years old—the same age when Martin Luther Jr. was murdered in 1968. Price's death at an early age meant that he was unable to write his biography similar to Washington and Douglass.
- Two blacks, Joe Kizer and Thomas Johnstone, were hanged near Concord because they allegedly cut the throat of Mr. Hartshell's

daughter from ear to ear in 1898. This was at the same time frame when Coleman was building his mill. The injustice of this case was never considered to remedy the pain caused by the behavior of a white mob.

- Price Memorial in Concord was financed and supported by Coleman in 1895 and beyond.

- Coleman and others from Zion Hill AME Zion Church made the payments to open a seventeen-acre cemetery known in 1876 as the Old Camp Ground Cemetery (OCGC). Presently, OCGC is suffering from neglect and lack of interest. Another cemetery in severe disrepair is the Lutheran cemetery, which is reserved for blacks, on Corban Avenue near the new jailhouse. The faith of the Lutheran black cemetery may be the faith of OCGC. The OCGC was recently mowed, but only half of the cemetery, due to anticipation of this book publication, was completed.

- Rufus Barringer later served as a trustee of Biddle College, which later changed its name to Johnson C. Smith University, a HBCU. It is also interesting to note that the first black president of Biddle College was Daniel Jackson Sanders, one of the people who assisted Coleman with the mill. The connection is very interesting.

- T. Thomas Fortune, due to several of his actions, has been considered to be a black radical, advocating violence in the same vein as Malcolm X in the 1960s. Fortune's posture may be why many people don't know him or the role he played in American history. MLK is preferred over Malcolm X.

- If he did not die in 1893, Price would have been selected as the new leader to replace Douglass, *not* Washington. Ida B. Wells was also considered for this leadership role.

- As of 1900 in America, Coleman was the richest black man in America. His wealth came in the form of his real estate holdings and family educational human capital and other tangible assets. It is also interesting to note that the richest black man in history was Mansa Musa of West Africa in the kingdom known as Mali in the fourteenth century.

- Douglass was honored in a similar manner as Lincoln and Grant when he (Douglass) passed away and laid out to be viewed by the people in New York City in 1895.
- The City of Tuskegee, Alabama, has done little to change the face of the city since the 1950s. However, Tuskegee University is well kept, and the people of America should be very proud of the legacy left by Washington. Unlike Barber-Scotia College, Tuskegee's legacy remains alive and well.
- The University of Tuskegee has over 180 buildings, and they are in reasonable condition for hundreds of students who attend from many parts of the country and the world. Compared to Barber-Scotia, Tuskegee is at the very height of black educational development in America. However, Morehouse College is considered at a higher level due to the number of Rhodes Scholars developed over the years. One of the youth from Price (Chance Barringer) was recently admitted. How he and his family might be connected to the white Barringers is another issue for another author.
- Washington and Coleman had a relationship, but it was not as close as the relationship between Fortune and Washington.
- The Coleman Mill in Concord, North Carolina, put together by Warren C. Coleman, was the first black textile manufacturing mills in America. Other black mills were developed in South Carolina; Durham, North Carolina; and Ocala, Florida. But Coleman's was the first. Has the town of Concord celebrated this fact? Yes and no.
- Coleman, in his efforts to operate a textile mill, was responding to the industrial revolution like the people of Europe and other parts of America. Coleman saw what was happening in the South and other parts of America, and he must have learned as much when he studied at a higher level at Howard University.
- Washington, in spite of their weak relationship, was offered the presidency of the mill by Coleman. Harlan, an author who has written extensively about Washington, indicated that Washington came to Concord. However, I could find no

evidence to support the idea that Washington came to Concord in the nineteenth or twentieth century.

- Even though Du Bois was a fierce critic of Washington, he had a closer relationship with Washington compared to Coleman, as referenced in the Washington Papers.

- Prior to the great Atlantic Exposition, there was a world's fair in Chicago in 1893; and blacks, for the most part, were excluded. People like Ida B. Wells voiced their outrage.

- The great leader of the anti-lynching movement, Ida B. Wells, was a mentor to W. E. B. Du Bois. Du Bois was one of the main founders of the NAACP, and Wells played a very significant role, more so than most people know. Wells was also being considered for the leadership role that was taken over by Washington.

- At the great Atlanta Exposition in 1895, Coleman was instrumental in helping people to attend by providing financial support where necessary. After returning from the exposition in 1895, Coleman decided to announce that a black textile mill would be developed in Concord in 1896. There is some controversy as to why Coleman decided to build the mill in 1896.

- Many people during that time, including Washington, thought that working in the mill was not lucrative or in the best interest of African-American men or women. Once Douglass passed away, Fortune became the kingmaker and agreed that Washington should be the new leader of black America.

- Price and Du Bois had similar feelings about race relations. Some people were sorry when Price passed away because Price and Du Bois would have been able to join together and speak the same language by advocating for equal treatment and rights for African-Americans in the North and South.

- The wealth that was developed by black men in 1896 for eight years was transferred to white men—Duke and Cannon. In this case, it is not a matter of reparations; it is a matter of paying the black community what black (with some help from whites) people built and with no real major tangible compensation. Mr. Cannon became a wealthy man on the wealth of plant no. 9.

How much wealth was generated from 1904 until the transfer of the deed to Mr. Bill Bryant? It would be wonderful to have a black museum in Concord to illustrate and highlight the history that took place by black men and women. The Coleman Mill would be an excellent choice. Ms. J. L. Anthony of Salisbury is trying to build a museum in her community. People from all the country and world would come to see this historic place similar to historic sites in Alabama, Mississippi, Atlanta, and other southern towns.

- There was one woman on the incorporation papers for the mill. Coleman wanted people on the incorporation papers who could later sell bonds/stocks and support the mill. Because black females did not have the same influence, more were not included, but they did play an important role.

- It is not clear why Coleman died in 1904, but stress must be included as one of the factors.

- Ms. Viola Barrett, an unsung, unassuming woman, has made a major difference in Concord and the Logan community. I had a chance to tell her this in June 2019 at the Logan Day Care Center. The City of Concord has agreed to work with blacks to acknowledge the past and the horrid details of slavery, but much more needs to be done. As we move into the future and minorities become the majority, it is also very important that the Cabarrus School Board take the steps necessary to encourage African-Americans to apply for the position. How could you be a legitimate body if there is no one on the board to speak for a very large part of the community (nonwhites)? And please don't tell me that whites can represent blacks after reading this book.

- The members of the Morrison family and their daughter (Coleman's half-sister by way of their father, Rufus Barringer) Eugene Morrison developed the great institution that is known as Davidson College. To substantiate this connection, after the Civil War, Rufus was seen selling land that was connected to Davidson College. The Morrisons are connected to Coleman and his father and his good friend, Dr. Joseph C. Price, who was instrumental in the development of Livingstone College. J. W. Hood was a mentor to both Coleman and Price. This legacy is awesome. Maybe one day there will be some form of acknowledgment about this incredible connection. Any additional information regarding the relationship between the Barringers and the Morrison family would be very interesting.

Concluding Statements

As I begin the conclusion of this book, I must say a few words about the four hundred years that black people have existed in America. How we acknowledge (not celebrate) this time, looking back, is important. It is important because black people have made significant strides in America in spite of the many obstacles. However, most of our time (close to 350 years of mistreatment) has seen blacks struggling to be free. One singer would say, "I wish I knew how it feels to be free" (Nina Simone). Are we now free? Sometimes I agree, and sometimes I don't. My main concern is that we have been programmed, and this programming comes in many forms. Three hundred and fifty years is a long time to be treated as third-class citizens or chattel slaves. Whether our children or their children will be truly free remains to be seen. As we approach 450 or 500 years of existence in America, let us all continue to make a difference for our youth like what Warren C. Coleman and many, many others have done. Given my seventy-three years of age, I tried my best to do my part. We all have a role to play.

As I look at all the various resources of information about the life and times of Warren C. Coleman, it is clear to me that his life is symbolic of life in America for African-Americans and many others. First and foremost, for many people in America who were born into slavery, like Frederick Douglass and Booker T. Washington, Coleman was able to rise above the status of a chattel slave and become a leader for the world to see.

To say that Coleman was the richest African-American in America as of 1900—from the standpoint of his material wealth and family background and accomplishment—is a major assertion in American history. Given this assertion, my challenge for anyone in the academic community is to prove that there is some other African-American similarly situated. Because of his own wealth and family's legal pedigree and religious training, Coleman was a giver. He gave to the people who needed to be buried in a dignified manner. Coleman decided in 1876, with the assistance of others from the Zion Hill Church, to make a way for others who could not make a way for themselves. He gave to the church, he gave to the community, and he gave to schools to ensure that young people could be encouraged to reach their maximum potential in spite of the legacy of Jim Crow. For the churches like Zion Hill and Price Memorial AME Zion, Coleman's contribution made a major difference. Unlike the AME community, the Zion community coming out of New York City (my hometown) became entrenched in North Carolina and other parts of the South. I have heard people in Price Memorial say that Coleman was a Zionite. I doubt very much if Coleman ever visited the John Street United Methodist Church, but his spirit must be there to enable me to find his church.

People like Mrs. Pearl Asbury, Mr. and Mrs. Thomas Dixon, Ms. Nancy Livingston, Mr. William Black and family, Mrs. Ella Mae Small, her late husband, Rev. Melvin McCullough, Mary Winecoff, Margaret Blue, Gloria A. Boulware, Eleanor Butler, and many others invested their lives in the church. Most recently, we lost another church giant, Mrs. Rosa Lee Weaks-Goins. There was standing room only at Price; as apparently, Mrs. Goins insisted that her services be held, in spite of the crowd overflow, at her historic church. Many of these people were former members of the church, and it is incumbent on the church to do everything possible to recapture this population moving into the future. Being able to accept new ideas to improve the church and ensure its growth is the name of the game. Given the end of discrimination on the basis of race and color in the 1950s, '60s, and the '70s in the South and the North, the AME Zion Church is struggling to attract new younger members to the Concord District. The irony of integration is that the church was much more vibrant under Jim Crow because the black community did not have many other options to attend church (see picture on page). In addition, the economics of our time, wherein religious leaders oftentimes must work in occupations outside the church, is also a major consideration for limited attention. One of reasons why the churches suffer is because many of the leaders can't afford to give the church his or her full attention. Working primarily for the church has become a luxury that most churches in the black community cannot afford. As such, in the past segregated churches were the norm, and membership was growing or at least remained the same. This recent lack of growth is an issue for people in the church, like me and others, that must be addressed. Writing this book has turned out to be one of my efforts in this regard.

As the leading black entrepreneur in the late 1800s, Coleman was clearly a man before his time. He was a leader who demonstrated that African-Americans could utilize their intellectual skills, come together, and meet a common objective. Their behavior and action was a clear example of black power before it was coined in the 1960s or fully implemented in 2008 with the election of Barack Obama. Obama was a leader who served America (blacks, whites, and others) for eight years without a major blemish, which is why many people (mostly white) needed to elect a man like Donald Trump. It should also be noted that Booker T. Washington indicated early in the 1900s that America would one day have a black president.

Coleman's wealth, based on evidence, was primarily based on the value of his real estate, his store, and other assets. However, getting the knowledge that was gleaned from his master (William Coleman) and his father (Rufus Barringer) put Coleman into the world of wealth that was unmatched by any other former slave in America in the late 1800s. Coleman was not the only African-American taking advantage of a newfound freedom to buy, sell, and manage real estate. However, he was the only one with the legal background and connections in North Carolina (how many other former slaves could say that their father was a mayor of a town in North Carolina?) to make it work for him to maximize his wealth. Those who could say their father was the president, like Thomas Jefferson, might have been in a similar position. However, in the case of President Jefferson, it is only recent that people have admitted, based on hard evidence, that our third president fathered six or seven children with Sally Hemings, a slave. Many of her children did not live long, and there have been several family reunions to demonstrate that the Jefferson family and the Hemings family are connected.

Given my journey on the learning curve, approaching the end and looking back, I feel truly blessed. For a young man, living and growing up in poverty in the projects of New York City, my life has been a true blessing. My life shows, without a doubt, that investing in education for blacks and whites can make a major difference in our society. Also living with God in mind and worshipping his every Word has made a major difference in life. My education was free except for some of my graduate education to obtain an EdD. As one great man stated, "We will reach the mountaintop." Another talked about seven habits of effective people; and another, my academic mentor, asserted that making a difference, person by person, is a great achievement for an educator. My great aunt (Lillian Mabel Barzey) would always say that with limited education, "Nothing happens before the time." And last but not least, another, a son of God, stated, "Love is more powerful than hate." Those who have loved me have changed the world. Imagine if my family members did not step in; I would now be dead, a victim of criminal justice system, or worse, strung out on drugs like many of my former neighbors in the Alfred E. Smith Houses. As God would have it, I was able to become a middle-level manager in the same NYC Housing Authority and retire in 2005. One of the managers in Smith Houses knew my story and would greet me with admiration every time she would see me in the development once I retired in 2005. And in 2012, I wrote my first book, *The Dream*. Peace, love, and happiness to all who have read my story and the story of African-Americans in the past and the present.

Bibliography

Manuscripts

North Carolina Office of Archives and History, University of North Carolina, Charlotte, North Carolina
Rufus Barringer Papers
John Barringer Papers
Paul Brandon Barringer Papers

Newspapers

February Conspectus
Cabarrus Neighbors
Cabarrus History
Charlotte Democrat
Charlotte Journal
Charlotte Observer
Chicken Hill, Asheville's newest old neighborhood
Chicago Tribune
Independent Tribune
Journal of Southern History
New York Times
North Carolina Daily Press
North Carolina Gazette
Raleigh State Chronicle

The Durham Recorder
The State Chronicle, Raleigh, North Carolina
Western Sentinel, Winston-Salem (1898)

Published Sources

Alexander, Roberta Sue, Rodney D. Barfield, and Steven E. Nash. "African Americans." 2006.

Banks, Kathryn M. Silva. "Six Days Thou Shall Labor." 2010.

Barringer, Sheridan R. *Fighting for General Lee: Confederate General Rufus Barringer and the North Carolina Cavalry Brigade.* 2016.

Blight, David W. and Frederick Douglass. *Prophet of Freedom.* Simon and Schuster, 2018.

Burgess, Allen Edward. "Tar Heel Blacks and the New South Dream: The Coleman Manufacturing Company, 1896–1904" (PhD diss., Duke University, 1977).

Coates, Eyler Robert, Sr. *The Jefferson-Hemings Myth: An American Travesty.* Charlottesville, VA: Thomas Jefferson Heritage Society, 2001.

Collins, Charles and David Cohen. *The African Americans.* Penguin Books, 1993.

Crow, Jeffrey J. *A History of African Americans in North Carolina.* 1992.

Davis, Bernard Jr. *Portraits of the African-American Experience in Concord-Cabarrus North Carolina, 1860–2008.* 2010.

Davis, Lenwood. "Dr. Joseph Charles Price an Unsung Hero."

Dortch, Thomas W., Jr. *The Miracles of Mentoring: How to Encourage and Lead Future Generations.* Random House, 2000.

Douglass, Frederick. *My Bondage and My Freedom.* Dover Publications, 1969.

Eury, Michael. *Legendary Locals of Cabarrus County.* 2015.

Franklin, John Hope. *Reconstruction after the Civil War.* Chicago, IL: University of Chicago Press, 1961.

Gates, Henry Louis, Jr. and Evelyn Brooks Higginbotham. *African American Lives.* Oxford University Press, 2004.

Gates, Henry Louis, Jr. *100 Amazing Facts about the Negro.* New York: Pantheon Books, 2017.

Harlan, Louis R. *Booker T. Washington: Up from Slavery.* 2009

Harlan, Louis R. *Booker T. Washington: Wizard of Tuskegee, 1901–1915*. 1983.

Harlan, Louis, R., ed. *The Booker T. Washington Papers* 1 and 4 (1975).

Harlan, Louis, R. *Booker T. Washington: The Making of a Black Leader, 1856–1901*. New York, 1972.

Hewitt, Nancy A. and Steven F. Lawson. *Exploring American Histories*, 3rd ed. Bedford/St. Martin's, 2019.

Hine, Darlene C., William Hine, and Stanley Harrold. *The African-American Odyssey*, 7th ed. 2018.

Hood, J. W. *One Hundred Years of the African Methodist Episcopal Zion Church*. 1895.

Horton, Clarence E. "History and Background of City of Concord: A Bicentennial Sketch."

Ingham, John N. and Lynne B. Feldman. *African-American Business Leaders: A Biographical Dictionary*.

Inscoe, John. "Price, Joseph Charles." 1994.

Johnson, Sallie R. "The Estate Record of Warren C. Coleman." 1904.

Judge, Edward H. and John W. Langdon. *Connections: A World History*, 3rd ed. 2016.

Judkins, Bennett M. and Dorothy Lodge. "The Evolution of Textile Mill Villages." 1986.

Leloudis, James. "Life in Textile Mill Villages." 1986.

Logan, Frenise A. *The Negro in North Carolina, 1876–1894*. Chapel Hill: University of North Carolina Press, 1964.

McGray, Carrie Allen. *Freedom's Child: The Life of a Confederate General's Black Daughter*. Chapel Hill: Algonquin Books, 1998.

Mclain, Denis. "Steward, Oppression by Omission, Race Before Gender and Education for Female Mill Workers." Historic Cabarrus Association Inc., 26, no. 2 (Summer 2018).

Mclain, Denis. "The Spirit of Concord's Logan High School Lives." July 13, 2015.

Minchin, Timothy. *Hiring the Black Worker: The Racial Integration of the Southern Textile Industry, 1960–1980*. University of North Carolina Press, 1999.

Minchin, Timothy. "Black Activism, the 1964 Civil Rights Act, and the Racial Integration of the Southern Textile Industry." *The Journal of Southern History* 65, no. 4.

Norrell, Robert J. *Up from History: The Life of Booker T. Washington.* Harvard University Press, 2009.

Gordon-Reed, Annette. *Thomas Jefferson and Sally Hemings: An American Controversy.* 1997.

Robinson, Harold O. *A History of African-Americans in Cabarrus County, North Carolina.* Concord, NC: Cabarrus County Bicentennial Commission, 1992.

Rouse, J. K. *The Noble Experiment of Warren C. Coleman.* Crabtree Press, 1972.

Simmons, William J. *Men of Mark, 1849–1890.* Durham Library.

Smith, Sam. "Black Confederates." American Battlefield Trust.

Thompson, Holland. *From the Cotton Field to the Cotton Mill: A Study of the Industrial Transition in North Carolina.* "The Rise of American Industry." USHistory.org.

Washington, Booker T. Booker T. An Autobiography. Barnes & Noble Inc., 1901.

Washington, Booker T. *The Story of the Negro, the Rise of the Race from Slavery* 2 (1909).

"33rd Annual Family and Friends Day," *Price Memorial Souvenir Journal* (March, 17, 2019).

Thesis

Krieger, Marvin. "Warren Clay Coleman, Promoter of the Black Cotton Mill: An Analysis of an Early Effort to Develop Black Economic Power" (master's thesis, Wake Forest University, 1969).

Speeches

Price, Joseph C. "Education and the Problem." Minneapolis, July 1890.

YouTube Video

Killer, Kimberly. "Old Camp Ground Cemetery." September 18, 2016.

Notes

Chapter One

1 Norman J. McCullough Sr., *The Dream: A Manual to Facilitate Group Mentoring and Prevent High School Dropouts for African-American, Hispanic and European-American Youth and Others in Need of Positive Role Models in Their Lives* (iUniverse, 2012), 4–8.

2 *Talented Tenth*—a term utilized by W. E. B. Du Bois to describe the elite of the African-American community in America. (See Robert J. Norrell's *Up from History*, 2009). However, the original person who coined the phrase was Henry L. Morehouse, a person that the famous college is named after according to Gates in *100 Amazing Facts about the Negro* (54).

3 "And still we rise" is a phrase utilized by author Maya Angelou when referring to the development of African-Americans in spite of the opposition of some whites.

4 Sheridan Barringer, *Fighting for General Lee: Confederate General Rufus Barringer and the North Carolina Cavalry Bridge* (Savas Beatie LLC, 2016), 30.

5 Booker Washington, *Up From Slavery*, 413.

6 Marvin Krieger, *Warren Coleman, Promoter of the Black Cotton Mill*, 38.

7 Ibid, 65.

8

Chapter Two

9 Clarence E. Horton Jr., "History and Background of Concord."

10 Henry Louis Gates, *100 Amazing Facts about the Negro*, 304.

11   Ibid, 60.

12   Annette Gordan-Reed, 166–168.

13   Heritage Society, *The Jefferson-Hemings Myth: An American Travesty*, 155.

14   J. K. Rouse, *The Noble Experiment of Warren C. Coleman*, 23

15   Helen Arthur, "Cabarrus Neighbor" (February 1992).

16   Ibid.

17   J. H. Williamson, *North-Carolina Gazette* (September 26, 1885).

18   Marvin Krieger, 35.

19   Bernard Davis Jr., *Portraits of the African-American Experience in Concord-Cabarrus, North Carolina*, 212.

Chapter Three

20   Sheridan Barringer, 30.

21   Ibid, 30.

22   J. K. Rouse, 21.

23   Sheridan Barringer, 38.

24   Ibid, 30.

25   Ibid, 30.

26   Kathryn L. Bridges, "Conspectus, Concord City Government—History of the Mayor's Office" (1993).

27   Wilford Kale, *Daily Press* (December 3, 2018).

28   Sheridan Barringer, 210.

29   Ibid, 215.

30   Ibid, 66.

31   Ibid, 259.

32   Ibid, 254.

33   Marvin Krieger, 272.

34   Ricky Riley, "6 Things You Should Know about Warren Clay Coleman, the Man Who Built the Country's First Black-Owned Textile Mill" (January 28, 2016).

35   Warren C. Coleman, February Conspectus (February 1988).

36   *Independent Tribune* 100, no. 164 (March 29, 2001).

37   Sam Smith, "Black Confederates: Truth and Legend" (American Battlefield Trust).

38   Darlene C. Hine, *The African-American Odyssey*, 304–306.

39   Sheridan Barringer, 12.

40 Ibid, 31.

41 Ibid, 265.

42 Carrie A. McCray, *Freedom's Child*, 23.

43 *The Charlotte Democrat* (February 2, 1877; March 27, 1876; August 3, 1894; and February 8, 1895).

44 Tuscarora Yarns Inc. Rev. Paul—not Warren's half-brother—incorporated a mill in 1889.

45 Robert Norrell, 233.

46 Harlan, 241.

47 Darlene Hine, 359.

48 Ibid, 384.

49 Ibid, 352.

50 Ibid, 484.

51 Henry Louis Gates, 865.

Chapter 4

52 Salley R. Johnson, "The Estate of Warren C. Coleman, Lots 1–57," Microfilm reel number 1685936.

53 North Carolina Industrial Association, State of the Chronicle (November 17, 1883) attended an exhibition with four cream-colored horses that were admired by everybody.

54 Frenise Logan, *The Negro in North Carolina 1876–1894*, 101.

55 Harold Robinson, *A History of African-Americans in Cabarrus County, North Carolina*, 93.

56 J. K. Rouse, 23.

57 Harold Robinson, 28–29.

58 Lenwood Davis, *The World's Orator: Selected Writings and Speeches of Joseph Charles Price, 1881–1893*.

59 One-page short history of Price Memorial AME Zion Church, see page.

60 Robert Norrell, 168.

61 Ibid, 415.

62 Ibid, 226.

Chapter Five

20–25 Pictures and documents

Chapter Six

63   Louis Harlan, Booker T. Washington: The Making of a Black Leader, 215.
64   Louis Harlan, ed., *Booker T. Washington Papers*, 98–99
65   Louis Harlan, *Booker T. Washington: The Making of a Black Leader*, 245.
66   Louis R. Harlan, *Booker T. Washington: The Wizard of Tuskegee, 1901–1915*, 431.
67   Louis Harlan, *Booker T. Washington Papers*, 413.
68   Henry Louis Gates, 852.
69   David W. Blight, 9.
70   Frederick Douglass, *My Bondage and My Freedom*, 35.
71   Ibid, 246.
72   Ibid, 81.
73   David W. Blight, 743.
74   Booker T. Washington, *Up from Slavery*, 123.
75   Robert Norrell, 132.
76   Henry Louis Gates, 851.
77   Joseph C. Price, "Education and the Problem" (1890).
78   Dr. Lenwood Davis, "Time for an Awakening" (February 12, 2013).
79   Hine, 444.
80   Robert J. Norrell, 132.
81   The *State Chronicle* (Raleigh, 1891).

Chapter Seven

82   Benneth M. Judkins and Dorothy Lodge (1986).
83   USHistory.org
84   Allen E. Burgess, 342.
85   Harlan, *Booker T. Washington Papers*, 98.
86   Helen Arthur (Sunday, April 11, 1999).
87   Ibid, 12K.
88   Coleman made a speech in front of the Old Concord Courthouse announcing that the mill would be built after returning from the Atlanta Exposition of 1896.
89   Robert Norrell, 490.
90   Benneth M. Judkins and Dorothy Lodge, "Evolution of Textile Mill Villages" (1986).
91   Chicken Hill, Asheville's newest old neighborhood.
92   Marvin Burgess, 215–234.

93 Harold Robinson, 146.

94 Marvin Krieger, 62.

95 Robert Norrell, 234.

96 Ms. Helen Arthur, *Charlotte Observer* (1992).

97 William Simmons, *Men of Mark* (GM Rewell & Co., 1887).

98 Kathryn M. Silva Banks, 154.

99 Ibid, 164.

100 Wikipedia, s.v. "Doffer in 1887."

101 Sheridan Barringer, 281.

102 Ibid, 281.

103 Helen Arthur, "A Man, a Dream, a Mill" (February 6, 1992).

104 David W. Blight, 553.

105 *Western Sentinel* (Winston-Salem, North Carolina, June 2, 1893).

106 Robert Norrell, 45 and 194.

107 Harlan, *Booker T. Washington Papers*, 99.

108 Darlene Clark Hine, 383.

109 Ibid, 385 and Robert Norrell, 179.

110 Allen Burgess, 344.

111 John Dancy, *AME Zion Quarterly Review*.

112 Burgess, 378.

113 Ibid, 374–376.

114 J. K. Rouse, 78.

115 Price Memorial Souvenir Booklet, 14.

116 Clarence E. Horton, "History and Background of Concord."

117 Wikepedia, s.v., "Black Billionaires."

118 Norman J. McCullough Sr., "Was Warren C. Coleman the Richest Black Man in America as of 1900?" (*Independent Tribune*, January 21, 2019, also see page).

119 Timothy Minchin, "Black Activism, the 1964 Civil Rights Act, and the Racial Integration of the Southern Textile Industry," *Journal of Southern History* 65, no. 4: 809.

Chapter Eight

120 See unveiling ceremony of the Warren C. Coleman Boulevard.

121 Michael Knox, "Tour Touches on Life, Accomplishments of Warren C. Coleman" (*Independent Tribune*, April 19, 2015).

122 Ibid.

123 *Independent Tribune,* see "John Price at OCGC," July 2016.

Chapter Nine

124 Thomas W. Dortch, The Miracles of Mentoring, 40–41.

125 Ibid, 52–55.

126 Michelle Alexander, *The New Jim Crow: Mass Incarceration in the Age of Colorblindness* (New York: New Press, 2012), 44, 84, and 192.

127 The first annual street fair took place on Union Street in Concord in conjunction with the City of Concord, North Carolina, in February 2018. Another proclamation celebrating Coleman was issued by the mayor and City of Concord in 2018 (see proclamation on page).

Index

Inside Cover

Warren C. Coleman, a son of Concord, North Carolina, was born a slave (like so many former slaves born in the South) and was destined to do nothing but survive and/or limit his contribution to society only as a chattel slave. Several other books have been written about Coleman, including a master's thesis by Marvin Krieger in 1969: "Warren Clay Coleman, Promoter of the Black Cotton Mill." However, my book is the first book written *exclusively* about Coleman by an African-American and a member of the African Methodist Episcopal Zion community. From this perspective, my book, highlighting the lives of his white family, hopefully can be a celebration of the life and times of a man (Coleman) before his time. I would also talk about men like Frederick Douglass, Booker T. Washington, Bishop J. W. Hood, Dr. Joseph C. Price, W. E. B. Du Bois, and many others too numerous to mention who made America what it is today and who are often unknown and unsung.

The record is clear that Coleman rose to be the richest African-American in America as of 1900. A part of his wealth had to do with various forms of real estate in Cabarrus County, North Carolina, and other counties in North Carolina—with the assistance of his white father and white master. Both were accomplished attorneys, and they trained Coleman in the real estate and the legal field. Moreover, Coleman collected rent from various properties that he owned and rented to close to three hundred black employees working in his newly developed textile mill. The mill was designed for employees who could not work in the 150 white mills in North Carolina. In addition to real estate and a mill, Coleman owned a grocery store where he serviced the needs of whites and blacks in Concord, North Carolina, in the late nineteenth century. In the rear of the store, he sold tar by the pint for fifteen cents. In light of his material wealth, Coleman was a man who gave to the African-Americans living and working in the surrounding community. The evidence strongly indicates that Coleman and his associates were designing a mill town (from Church Street down to Depot [now Cabarrus], down to Old Charlotte Road, to Highway 601, and around to Lincoln Street) where people could eat, work, go to school, be buried, and go to church. Whites did not live alongside blacks in those days, and they did not worship together. For example, Coleman was a member of Zion Hill AME Zion Church (located on Depot Street), and he did whatever was necessary to financially support the church. The church was located very close to Scotia College.

However, in 1895, with the support of several other members, he decided to finance and develop what was known as Price Temple, later changed to Price Memorial AME Zion Church in Concord, North Carolina. Price Memorial, celebrating over 123 years of existence, remains a very active church today; and I have been privileged to be one of its trustees for several years. Coleman also made it possible for African-Americans to be buried in a seventeen-acre cemetery known as Old Camp Ground Cemetery, currently owned by Zion Hill AME Zion Church, and to work in a 196,000 square foot manufacturing mill. Both remain intact today. This remarkable new biography teaches us many things. First and foremost is the point that all of us must continue the reconciliation process so that the damage of close to 250 years of slavery and 100 years of Jim Crow can be resolved in a manner that helps to preserve the United States of America as a racially diverse country that will grow and prosper into the future.